博雅国际汉语精品教材

汉语初级强化教程·综合课本 I（第二版）

Intensive Elementary Chinese Course

A Comprehensive Book I
Second Edition

肖奚强　朱　敏　主编

北京大学出版社

图书在版编目 (CIP) 数据

汉语初级强化教程. 综合课本. I / 肖奚强，朱敏主编. —2版 —北京：北京大学出版社，2020.9
博雅国际汉语精品教材
ISBN 978-7-301-31526-2

Ⅰ.①汉…　Ⅱ.①肖…②朱…　Ⅲ.①汉语－对外汉语教学－教材　Ⅳ.①H195.4

中国版本图书馆 CIP 数据核字（2020）第 150507 号

书　　　名	汉语初级强化教程·综合课本 I（第二版） HANYU CHUJI QIANGHUA JIAOCHENG · ZONGHE KEBEN I (DI-ER BAN)
著作责任者	肖奚强　朱　敏　主编
责任编辑	唐娟华
美术制作	张婷婷
标准书号	ISBN 978-7-301-31526-2
出版发行	北京大学出版社
地　　　址	北京市海淀区成府路 205 号　100871
网　　　址	http://www.pup.cn　新浪微博：@北京大学出版社
电子信箱	zpup@pup.cn
电　　　话	邮购部 010-62752015　发行部 010-62750672　编辑部 010-62767349
印 刷 者	三河市博文印刷有限公司
经 销 者	新华书店 889 毫米 × 1194 毫米　大16开本　18.75 印张　372 千字 2008 年 5 月第 1 版 2020 年 9 月第 2 版　2024 年 3 月第 3 次印刷
定　　　价	76.00 元

未经许可，不得以任何方式复制或抄袭本书之部分或全部内容。
版权所有，侵权必究
举报电话：010-62752024　电子信箱：fd@pup.pku.edu.cn
图书如有印装质量问题，请与出版部联系，电话：010-62756370

修订说明

《汉语初级强化教程》系列教材自2008年陆续出版至今已有十多个年头了。与之配套的、启动于2005年的教学改革（将独立开课的听、说、读、写四门课整合为相互配合的听说、读写两门课）于2009年获得南京师范大学优秀教学成果特等奖。我们在保持原有教材综合与听说相结合、结构与功能相结合、语言与文化相结合的基本编写原则的基础上，结合编写团队来自教学的反思以及出版社从使用单位收集到的反馈意见，主要从以下几个方面对教材进行了修订和完善。

第一，增加了表现新事物新现象的新词语。如"微信、快递、二维码、支付宝、共享单车"等。

第二，删除过时的话题和课文内容，代之以更能反映当前社会生活的话题和内容。如"支付方式不仅可以使用现金，还可以使用微信和支付宝等其他方式"。

第三，根据词语和话题的变动，适当调整语言点的安排，以使语言点的前后照应、循序渐进以及注释更加完善。

第四，练习形式更加多样。如听说课本增加了与HSK题型相一致的练习，增加了交际型练习。

第五，订正了原教材中的错漏。

第六，为了突出教学重点，适当调整了教材的板块和版式设计，改用双色印刷，设计装帧更加美观，以提高学生学习汉语的兴趣。

教材修订者基本为原班人马。梁社会承担了他本人参编的36—40课的修订工作；范伟因为另有任务，未能参加修订工作，她编写的内容由周文华负责修订；其他人员承担了各自编写内容的修订工作；最后全书的修订稿由肖奚强统筹定稿。

希望第二版能够继续受到汉语教学界的欢迎。同时也希望能够得到使用本教材的专家学者的批评指正。

肖奚强

2020年9月

前言 PREFACE

对外汉语初级教材经过多年的建设,已经取得了相当的成绩,比如:教材的数量以较快的速度增长,教材的种类不断丰富;教材编写的理论研究和经验总结也不断深入和加强等。但是,已有的初级汉语系列教材在教学内容、教学重点、结构、功能和文化的相互配合,课程之间的相互配套等方面还有许多需要改进的方面。因此,我们从教学实践出发,编写了《汉语初级强化教程》系列教材,希望能够为初级汉语教材建设添砖加瓦。

编写本套教材的基本原则为三个结合:综合与听说相结合、结构与功能相结合、语言与文化相结合。

一 综合汉语教材与听说教材的课文,在内容和形式上密切配合,相互补充,注重词汇和语法点的互现和循环。全套教材由一套人马统一编写,避免两种教材众人分头编写、相互不配套、难以施教的现象。

二 针对目前初级汉语教学中听力和口语分别开课,两门课的教材、教学内容不配套现象严重(或互不相干,或重复重叠)的现状,将听和说整合为一本教材、一门课,改变听说分课、教材不配套、教学相互抵牾的状况。

三 注重结构、功能、文化的结合,以结构为主线,辅以交际功能,穿插文化背景介绍;增强教材的知识性、实用性和趣味性。

四 教材中的所有词汇、语法点均与汉语水平考试大纲、对外汉语教学大纲相对照,确保词汇、语法学习的循序渐进,尽可能避免生词、语法的超纲。当然,对于学生学习、交际急需而现行大纲缺少或等级较高的词语,我们也本着实用的原则,酌情加入。

五 本套系列教材的所有编写人员均参与教材的试用,直接吸收教学中的反馈意见,并在四个平行班试用两年的基础之上进行了修改完善。

本套系列教材按《汉语初级强化教程·综合课本》《汉语初级强化教程·听说课本》分课编写,主要供汉语言专业本科生、进修生和汉语预科生一学年使用(建议综合课与听说课之比为5:4)。为了便于不同起点的班级选用,我们将上下学期使用的《汉语初级强化教程·综合课本》《汉语初级强化教程·听说课本》各分为两册,即综合课本和听说课本各为4册。

本教程由主编提出整体构想和编写原则与大纲，编写组讨论完善后分头编写。具体分工如下：

朱敏编写综合课本1—6课、41—45课，听说课本1—5课、41—45课。

沈灿淑编写综合课本7—12课、46—50课，听说课本6—8课、10—12课、46—50课。

范伟编写综合课本13—16课、25课、51—55课，听说课本9课、13—16课、19课、25课、51—55课。

段轶娜编写综合课本17—22课、56—60课，听说课本17课、18课、20—22课、56—60课。

魏庭新编写综合课本、听说课本的23课、24课、26—28课、30课、61—65课。

张勤编写综合课本、听说课本的29课、31—35课，66—70课。

梁社会与沈灿淑合编综合课本、听说课本第36课，与范伟合编第37、38课，与魏庭新合编第39课，与张勤合编第40课。

全书由主编修改定稿。

本套系列教材从策划、编写、试用到出版历时两年有余。从2005年9月至2007年6月在南京师范大学国际文化教育学院理工农医经贸专业汉语预科生的四个平行班试用了两学年。教学效果良好，从形式到内容都受到留学生的欢迎和好评。作为听说合一、综合课与听说课密切配合编写教材的一种尝试，不足之处在所难免。希望得到专家学者和使用本教材同行的批评指正。

编　者

2008年

目录 CONTENTS

现代汉语语音发音要领 ... 1

第 一 课	你好	17
第 二 课	汉语难吗	33
第 三 课	今天星期几	44
第 四 课	这是什么	57
第 五 课	复习（一）	70
第 六 课	我们都喜欢汉语	79
第 七 课	你们班有多少个学生	91
第 八 课	请问，留学生食堂在哪儿	104
第 九 课	没有课的时候，你做什么	118
第 十 课	复习（二）	131
第十一课	一斤多少钱	139
第十二课	你的生日是什么时候	152
第十三课	你最近学习怎么样	167
第十四课	我们坐地铁去吧	184
第十五课	复习（三）	200
第十六课	晚上听听音乐，看看电视	208
第十七课	地铁站在哪儿	223
第十八课	我不会画画儿	239
第十九课	我不喜欢在网上买衣服	255
第二十课	复习（四）	270

生词索引 ... 279

语法索引 ... 288

现代汉语语音发音要领
Main Points of Modern Chinese Pronunciation

一 声母的发音 Pronunciation of Initials

b [p] 双唇不送气清塞音。双唇闭合,阻塞气流,然后突然张开嘴,较弱的气流爆发而出。声带不振动。

Unaspirated voiceless bilabial plosive. Lung air is compressed by the closure of both lips. Then the air escapes with a sudden release of the lips opening, with no vibrations of the vocal cords.

p [pʰ] 双唇送气清塞音。发音情况和 b 基本一致,只是进出的气流较强。

Aspirated voiceless bilabial plosive. The position of pronunciation is the same as that of b, yet the air released is stronger.

m [m] 双唇浊鼻音。双唇闭合,软腭和小舌下垂,气流从鼻腔出来。声带振动。

Voiced bilabial nasal. The lips close, and the soft palate and the uvula are lowered. The air passes through the nasal cavity, with vibrations of the vocal cords.

f [f] 唇齿清擦音。上齿轻触下唇,中间留一条缝隙;气流从缝隙中摩擦而出。声带不振动。

Voiceless labiodental fricative. The upper teeth make a light contact with the lower lip and the air is released in between with a friction, with no vibrations of the vocal cords.

d [t] 舌尖中不送气清塞音。舌尖抵住上齿龈,阻塞气流,然后突然打开,较弱的气流爆发成音。

Unaspirated voiceless alveolar plosive. The tongue tip is pressed against the upper alveolar ridge so as to compress the air inside the oral cavity. Then release the air suddenly so that the weak air stream makes a sound.

t [tʰ] 舌尖中送气清塞音。发音情况和 d 基本一致,只是进出的气流较强。

Aspirated voiceless alveolar plosive. Its position of pronunciation is almost the same as d, only the air released is much stronger.

n [n] 舌尖中浊鼻音。舌尖顶住上齿龈,软腭和小舌下垂,气流从鼻腔中出来。声带振动。

Voiced alveolar nasal. The tongue tip is pressed against the upper alveolar ridge, the soft palate and uvula are lowered, and the air is released through the nasal cavity, with vibrations of the vocal cords.

l [l] 舌尖中浊边音。舌尖抵住上齿龈,但舌头两侧留有空隙,气流从两边空隙中流出。

声带振动。

Voiced alveolar lateral. The tongue tip is pressed against the upper alveolar ridge, with gas on both sides of the tongue, from which the air is released, with vibrations of the vocal cords.

g [k] 舌根不送气清塞音。舌根抬起抵住软腭，形成阻塞，然后突然离开，较弱的气流爆发成音。声带不振动。

Unaspirated voiceless velar plosive. The back of the tongue is raised and pressed against the soft palate to prevent the air. Then release the air suddenly and the weak air stream escapes, with no vibrations of the vocal cords.

k [kʰ] 舌根送气清塞音。发音情况和 g 基本一致，但是进出气流较强。

Aspirated voiceless velar plosive. The position of pronunciation is almost the same as g, yet the air released is much stronger.

h [x] 舌根清擦音。舌根抬起靠近软腭，中间留一条窄窄的缝隙，气流从缝隙中摩擦而出。声带不振动。

Voiceless velar fricative. The back of the tongue is raised towards the soft palate, with only a narrow gap in between. The air is expelled, causing some frictions in the vocal tract, with no vibrations of the vocal cords.

j [tɕ] 舌面不送气清塞擦音。发音时，舌面前部抬起，顶住硬腭前部，舌尖抵住下齿背；软腭和小舌上升，堵住鼻腔通路；较弱的气流从舌面与硬腭前部形成的缝隙中摩擦而出。声带不振动。

Unaspirated voiceless palatal affricate. The front part of the tongue is raised to the front of the hard palate. The tongue tip is pressed against the back of the lower teeth. The soft palate and uvula rise to obstruct the nasal. A weak air is squeezed out through the passage between the front part of the tongue and the hard palate, with no vibrations of the vocal cords.

q [tɕʰ] 舌面送气清塞擦音。发音情况和 j 基本一致，但是在除阻时，有一股较强的气流克服舌面和硬腭前部形成的阻碍，即要尽量送气。

Aspirated voiceless palatal affricate. Its position is the same as that of j, but in breaking the obstruct, a strong air overcomes the obstruct formed by the front part of the tongue and the hard palate, so it requires strong aspiration.

x [ɕ] 舌面清擦音。发音时，舌面前部抬起，靠近硬腭前部；软腭和小舌上升，堵住鼻腔通路；气流从舌面前部与硬腭前部的窄缝中摩擦而出，但声带不振动。

Voiceless palatal fricative. The front part of the tongue is raised to a position near the front of the hard palate. The soft palate and uvula rise to obstruct the nasal. The air stream is released in between with a friction, with no vibrations of the vocal cords.

z [ts] 舌尖前不送气清塞擦音。发音时，舌尖顶住上齿背，然后舌尖移开些，让较弱的气流从舌尖和上齿背的缝隙中摩擦而出，但声带不振动，形成先塞后擦的发音。

Unaspirated voiceless frontal-alveolar affricate. First the front part of the tongue is pressed against the upper alveolar ridge, then the tongue tip moves apart to let out the air stream through the narrow passage, with no vibrations of the vocal cords.

c [tsʰ] 舌尖前送气清塞擦音。发音情况和 z 基本一致，但在除阻时要尽量送气。

Aspirated voiceless frontal-alveolar affricate. Its position of pronunciation is the same as that of z, but it requires strong aspiration.

s [s] 舌尖前清擦音。舌尖靠近上齿背，中间留一条窄窄的缝隙，然后气流从舌尖和上齿背形成的窄缝中摩擦而出，但声带不振动。

Aspirated frontal-alveolar fricative. The tongue tip makes a light contact with the back of upper teeth to form a narrow gap. The air stream is squeezed out between the tongue tip and the back of the upper teeth, with no vibrations of the vocal cords.

zh [tʂ] 舌尖后不送气清塞擦音。舌尖上翘，抵住硬腭，然后较弱的气流从舌尖与硬腭形成的缝隙中摩擦而出，但不振动声带，形成先塞后擦的发音。

Unaspirated voiceless post-alveolar affricate. The tongue tip rises against the hard palate to form a narrow gap, and then weak air stream is let out through the gap, with no vibrations of the vocal cords.

ch [tʂʰ] 舌尖后送气清塞擦音。发音情况和 zh 基本一致，但除阻时，要尽量送气。

Aspirated voiceless post-alveolar affricate. Its position of pronunciation is the same as that of zh, but it is aspirated.

sh [ʂ] 舌尖后清擦音。舌尖上翘，靠近硬腭，然后气流从舌尖和硬腭形成的窄缝中摩擦而出，但声带不振动。

Voiceless post-alveolar affricate. The tongue tip is raised close to the hard palate to form a narrow gap, and the air stream is let out through the gap, with no vibrations of the vocal cords.

r [ʐ] 舌尖后浊擦音。发音情况和 sh 基本一致，不过是浊音，气流通过喉头时要振动声带。

Voiced post-alveolar affricate. Its position of pronunciation is the same as that of sh, it is voiced. The vocal cords vibrate when the air stream passes through.

以下是上述声音的发音情况图：
The following are the sketches maps of the above initials:

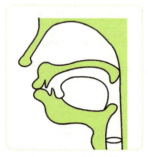

图 1　声母 b、p 的发音
Pronunciation of the initials b and p

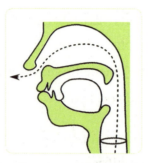

图 2　声母 m 的发音
Pronunciation of the initial m

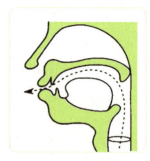

图 3　声母 f 的发音
Pronunciation of the initial f

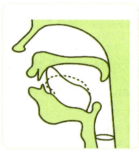

图 4　声母 d、t 的发音
Pronunciation of the initials d and t

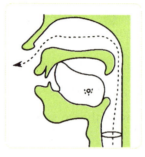

图 5　声母 n 的发音
Pronunciation of the initial n

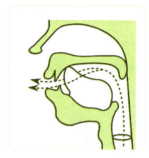

图 6　声母 l 的发音
Pronunciation of the initial l

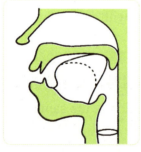

图 7　声母 g、k 的发音
Pronunciation of the initials g and k

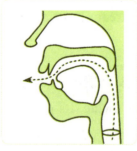

图 8　声母 h 的发音
Pronunciation of the initial h

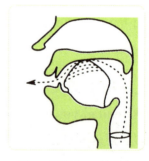

图 9　声母 j、q 的发音
Pronunciation of the initials j and q

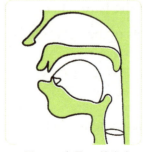

图 10　声母 x 的发音
Pronunciation of the initial x

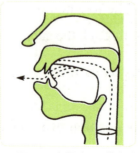

图 11　声母 z、c 的发音
Pronunciation of the initials z and c

图 12　声母 s 的发音
Pronunciation of the initial s

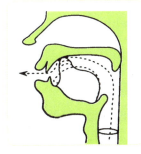
图 13 声母 zh、ch 的发音
Pronunciation of the initials zh and ch

图 14 声母 sh 的发音
Pronunciation of the initial sh

图 15 声母 r 的发音
Pronunciation of the initial r

（以上各图采自李振麟《发音基础知识》
All the graphs above are cited from *Basic Pronunciation* by Li Zhenlin）

二 韵母的发音 Pronunciation of Finals

1. 单元音韵母的发音 Pronunciation of simple-vowel finals

每一个元音都可以从舌头的高低、前后以及嘴唇的圆展三个方面来加以描述。下面是普通话 7 个舌面元音的发音示意图及发音要领描述：

Every vowel can be described by the tongue position (high, low, front and back) and how much the lips are rounded. The following is the description to the pronunciation graphs of the seven blade vowels in Mandarin.

a [ʌ]　央、低、不圆唇元音。口腔大开，舌位降到最低，唇形自然、不圆。

Central, low, unrounded-lip vowel. The mouth is widely open, the tongue is lowest, and the lips are not rounded.

o [o]　后、半高、圆唇元音。口腔半闭，舌头后缩，舌位半高、偏后，唇形圆。

Back, half-high, round-lip vowel. Mouth half-opened, tongue mid-high and slightly to the back, with rounded lips.

e [ɤ]　后、半高、不圆唇元音。口腔半闭，舌头后缩，舌位半高，嘴角向两边展开，唇形不圆。e 和 o 的发音基本相同，区别仅在嘴唇的圆展。

Back, half-high, unrounded-lip vowel. Mouth half-opened, tongue mid-high and slightly to the back, and the lips unrounded, mouth-ends spread. Its pronunciation description is almost the same as that of o, the only difference lies in whether the lips are round or spread.

i [i]　前、高、不圆唇元音。开口度很小，舌头前伸，舌位最高，嘴角向两边展开呈扁平状。

Front, high, unrounded-lip vowel. Mouth slightly-opened, the tongue is highest and positioned forward. Mouth-ends spread to both sides.

u [u]　后、高、圆唇元音。开口度很小，舌头后缩，舌位最高，嘴唇拢圆。

Back, high, rounded-lip vowel. Mouth is slightly open, tongue is highest and positioned back, the lips are rounded.

ü [y]　前、高、圆唇元音。开口度很小，舌头前伸，舌位最高，嘴唇拢圆。ü和i的发音情况基本差不多，不同的也只是嘴唇的圆和不圆。

Front, high, rounded-lip vowel. Mouth slightly-opened, tongue to the front but at the highest position, the lips round. It is similar to that of i, the difference lies in whether the lips are rounded or not.

-i [ɿ]　舌尖前、高、不圆唇元音。它只出现在声母 z、c、s 后面，不单独发音，可以认为是这三个辅音的延续。发音时舌尖前伸，对着上齿背，但中间有缝隙。

The tongue tip rises forward and high, and the lips are unrounded. It only follows the initials z, c and s, therefore it may be regarded as the extention of the three initials. When it is pronounced, the tongue tip is raised forward to the back of upper teeth, but with a gap in between.

-i [ʅ]　舌尖后、高、不圆唇元音。它只出现在声母 zh、ch、sh、r 后面，不单独发音，可以认为是这四个辅音的延续。发音时舌尖上翘，对着硬腭最前端，但中间有缝隙。

The tongue tip position is at back and high. The lips are unrounded. It only follows zh, ch, sh and r, so it cannot pronounced alone. It may be regarded as the extension of the four initials. When it is pronounced, the tongue tip is raised against the very front of hard palate, but with a gap in between.

注意：-i [ɿ] 和 -i [ʅ] 一定不能读成 [i]。

Note：-i [ɿ] and -i [ʅ] can't be pronounced as [i].

er [ɚ]　央、中、不圆唇卷舌元音。发音时先把舌头放在 e 的位置，然后在将舌尖轻轻上翘的同时发音。

It is a medium, mid-high with unrounded-lips. First put the tongue in the position for e, then when pronouncing er, slightly curl up the tongue tip.

下面是这些单韵母的发音舌位图：
The following are the tongue positions of these simple finals:

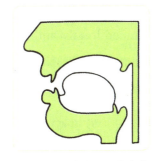
图 16　单韵母 a 的发音
Pronunciation of the simple final a

图 17　单韵母 o 的发音
Pronunciation of the simple final o

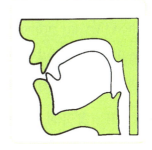
图 18　单韵母 e 的发音
Pronunciation of the simple final e

图 19　单韵母 i 的发音
Pronunciation of the simple final i

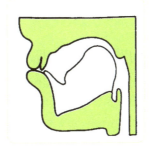
图 20　单韵母 u 的发音
Pronunciation of the simple final u

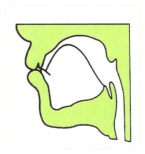
图 21　单韵母 ü 的发音
Pronunciation of the simple final ü

图 22　单韵母 -i[ɿ] 的发音
Pronunciation of the simple final -i[ɿ]

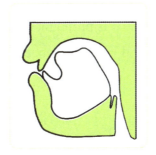
图 23　单韵母 -i[ʅ] 的发音
Pronunciation of the simple final -i[ʅ]

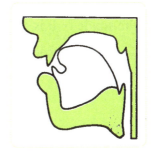
图 24　单韵母 er[ɚ] 的发音
Pronunciation of the simple final er

2. 复元音韵母的发音　Pronunciation of Compound-vowel Finals

复元音韵母发音时，嘴唇和整个共鸣器的形状要发生变化。

To pronounce the compound-vowel finals, the lips and the shapes of the whole resonator change.

（1）前响复韵母 ai、ei、ao、ou 的发音
Pronunciation of front-sound compound-vowel finals ai, ei, ao, ou

发音时，前一个成分 a-、e-、a-、o- 响亮、清晰，是韵腹；后一个成分 -i、-i、-o、-u 轻短模糊，音值不固定，它们只表示发音时舌位滑动的方向。下面分别对它们的发音情况加以描述：

When they are pronounced, the front elements a-, e-, a-, o- are pronounced loudly and clearly, they are the cores of the finals; the back elements -i, -i, -o, -u are pronounced lightly, shortly and vague, with unfixed syllable weight. The following are the descriptions of their pronunciation:

ai [ai] 发音时由 a 向 i 过渡。a 的实际读音比 a 单独读时舌位稍高，发音响亮清晰；i 的实际读音比 i 单独念时舌位稍低，发音轻短。

It is pronounced from a to i. The tongue position of the actual a is higher than the single a, and it is pronounced loudly and clearly. The tongue position of the actual i is lower than the single i, and it is pronounced lightly and shortly.

ei [ei] 发音时由 e 向 i 过渡。e 的发音响亮清晰，i 发音轻短。

It is pronounced from e to i. e is pronounced loudly and clearly, while i is pronounced lightly and shortly.

ao [au] 发音时由 a 向 o 过渡。a 的实际读音比 a 单独读时舌位靠后，是个后低元音，发音响亮清晰；o 的实际读音比 o 单独念时舌位稍低，发音轻短，音值模糊。

It is pronounced from a to o. The tongue position of the real sound is a little bit backward than that of the single a. It is a back-low vowel. It is pronounced loudly and clearly; The tongue position of actual o is lower than the single one, and it is pronounced lightly and shortly, with vague syllable weight.

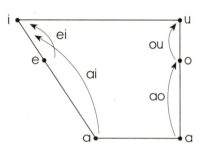

图 25 前响复韵母舌位示意图
Front-sound compound-vowel finals

ou [əu] 发音时由 o 向 u 过渡。o 的实际读音比 o 单独读时舌位稍稍靠前，圆唇度也较低，发音响亮清晰；u 的发音轻短，音值模糊。

It is pronounced from o to u. The tongue position of the actual sound o is a little bit forward than that of a single o, and the lips are not so round. It is pronounced loudly and clearly, while u is pronounced lightly and shortly, with vague syllable weight.

(2) 后响复韵母 ia、ie、ua、uo、üe 的发音
Pronunciation of back-sound compound-vowel finals ia, ie, ua, uo, üe

发音时，后一个元音比前一个元音清晰响亮；前面的元音发音轻短，只表示复韵母发音

时开始的位置。下面分别对它们的发音情况加以描述：

When they are pronounced, the back vowels are pronounced louder and clearer than the former ones. The former vowels are pronounced lightly and shortly, which only indicate the starting position of the compound finals. The following are the descriptions of their pronunciation：

ia [iA]　发音时由 i 向 a [A] 过渡。i 的读音轻而短，a 的读音为央低元音 [A]，发音时间长，响亮清晰。

It is pronounced from i to a [A]. i is pronounced lightly and shortly, and a is pronounced as the central low vowel [A], long, loudly and clearly.

ie [iɛ]　发音时由 i 向 ê[ɛ] 过渡。i 的读音轻而短，舌位稳定，和 i 单念时保持一致。e 的舌位较前半低元音 ê[ɛ] 稍高，发音时间长，响亮清晰。例如：yē（耶）、jié yè（结业）。

It is pronounced from i to ê[ɛ]。i is pronounced lightly and shortly, with steady tongue position，just the same as to pronounce the single i. The tongue position of e is a little higher than the front half low vowel ê[ɛ]. It is pronounced long, loudly and clearly, e.g. yē, jié yè.

ua [uA]　发音时由 u 向 a [A] 过渡。u 的读音轻而短，舌位稳定，和 u 单念时保持一致。a 的读音为央低元音 [A]，发音时间长，响亮清晰。

It is pronounced from u to a [A]. u is pronounced lightly and shortly, with steady tongue position, the same as to pronounce the single u. a is pronounced as the central low vowel [A], long, loudly and clearly.

uo [uo]　发音时由 u 向 o [o] 过渡。u 的读音轻而短，舌位稳定，和 u 单念时保持一致。o 的发音时间长，响亮清晰。

It is pronounced from u to o [o]. u is pronounced lightly and shortly with steady tongue position, the same as to pronounce the single u. o is pronounced long, loudly and clearly.

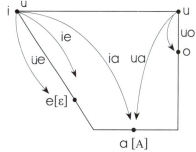

图 26　后响复韵母舌位示意图
Back-sound compound-vowel finals

üe [yɛ]　发音时由 ü 向 e[ɛ] 过渡。ü 的读音轻而短，舌位稳定，和 ü 单念时保持一致。e 的舌位较前半低元音 ê[ɛ] 稍高，发音时间长，响亮清晰，略带圆唇。

It is pronounced from ü to e[ɛ]. ü is pronounced lightly and shortly, with steady tongue position，the same as to pronounce the single ü. The tongue position of e is a little higher than the front half low vowel ê[ɛ]. It is pronounced long, loudly and clearly, with little round lips.

（3）中响复韵母 iao、iou、uai、uei 的发音
Pronunciation of mid-sound compound-vowel finals iao, iou, uai, uei

发音时，中间的元音最响，前边比较弱，后面的元音发音短轻，音值不固定，只表示舌位滑动的方向。下面分别对它们的发音情况加以描述：

When they are pronounced, the mid vowels are loudest, the former ones are weaker, and the back ones are short and light, with unfixed syllable weight, only indicating the orientation of the moving tongue. The following are the descriptions of their pronunciation：

iao [iau]　iao 由韵头 i 加前响复韵母 ao 构成。发音时韵头 i 和 i 单念时保持一致，但读得很短，舌位稳定。ao 的读音同前响复韵母 ao。

iao consists of the final head i and the front-sound compound final ao. When it is pronounced, the final head is pronounced the same as the single i, but very short, with steady tongue position. The pronunciation of ao is the same as that of the front-sound compound final ao.

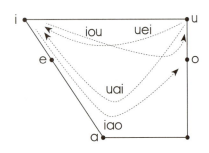

图 27　中响复韵母舌位示意图
Mid-sound compound-vowel finals

iou [iəu]　iou 由韵头 i 加前响复韵母 ou 构成。发音时韵头 i 和 i 单念时保持一致，但读得很短，舌位稳定。韵腹 o 比在前响复韵母 ou 中读得短。舌位先降低再升高，由前到后，变化幅度较小。

iou consists of the final head i and the front-sound compound final ou. It is pronounced the same as the single i, but very short, with steady tongue position. o, the core is pronounced shorter than that in the front-sound compound final ou. The tongue position falls down first and then rise, from front to back, but within the limited range.

uai [uai]　uai 由韵头 u 加前响复韵母 ai 构成。发音时韵头 u 和 u 单念时保持一致，但读得很短，舌位稳定。ai 的读音同前响复韵母 ai。

uai consists of the final head u and the front-sound compound final ai. The final head u is pronounced the same as the single u, but very short, with steady tongue position. ai is pronounced the same as the front-sound compound final ai.

uei [uei]　uei 由韵头 u 加前响复韵母 ei 构成。发音时韵头 u 和 u 单念时保持一致，但读得很短，舌位稳定。韵腹 e 比在前响复韵母 ei 中读得短。舌位先降低再升高，由前到后，变化幅度较小。

uei consists of u, the final head and ei, the front-sound compound final. The final head u is pronounced the same as the single u, but very short, with steady tongue position. e, the core is pronounced shorter than that in ei. The tongue position falls down first and then rise, from front to back, but within the limited range.

3. 鼻韵母的发音　Pronunciation of the nasal finals

（1）-n 和 -ng 的发音
Pronunciation of -n, -ng

汉语中，由一个或两个元音带上鼻辅音 -n 或 -ng 构成的韵母叫鼻音韵母。带 -n 的叫前鼻音韵母；带 -ng 的叫后鼻音韵母。

In Chinese, a final consisting of one or two vowels with a nasal -n or -ng is called the nasal final. The one with -n is called the front nasal final and the one with -ng is called the back nasal final.

带 -n 的前鼻韵母发音时，先发元音，接着舌尖向上齿龈移动，并抵住上齿龈，同时软腭逐渐下降，打开鼻腔通道。当气流从鼻腔共鸣流出时，舌尖与齿龈不解除阻碍，鼻音已发完了。

When a front nasal final is pronounced, the vowel is pronounced first, and then the tongue tip is pressed against the upper alveolar ridge, the soft palate are lowed gradually, and the air is let out through the nasal cavity, keeping the pressed position of the tongue tip and the upper alveolar ridge. In this way, the nasal final is pronounced.

带舌根音 -ng 的后鼻音韵母发音时，先发元音，紧接着舌根部分上抬，与软腭形成阻碍，同时软腭下垂，挡住气流通往口腔的道路，此时，舌尖应下垂，不可能接触到上齿龈。当气流从鼻腔流出时，舌根与软腭不解除阻碍，这个音已经发完了。

When a back nasal final with -ng is pronounced, the vowel is pronounced first, and then the back of the tongue is lifted to the soft palate and meanwhile, the soft palate are lowed so as to prevent the air to pass through the mouth. The tongue tip is lowed and not pressed against the upper alveolar ridge. When the air is let out through the nasal cavity, keeping the position of the back of the tongue and the soft palate. In this way, the nasal final is pronounced.

应该注意的是，韵母中的鼻音与做声母的鼻音发音时略有不同，发音结束时舌头必须依然停留在鼻辅音的发音部位，这是检验鼻韵母发音是否准确的标准之一。

It ought to be pointed out that there is slight difference between the nasal finals and the nasal initials. When the nasal final is pronounced over, the tongue must be at the original pronunciation position of that nasal final. It is one of the standards to check whether the nasal final is pronounced right or not.

下面是 -ng 的发音示意图：
The following is the figure of -ng pronunciation:

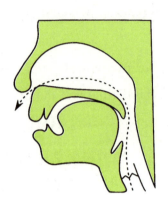

(2) an、ang；en、eng；ong 中 a、e、o 的发音
The pronunciation of a, e and o in an, ang; en, eng; ong

汉语拼音方案中只有 a、o、e、i、u、ü 六个元音字母，可是普通话中的元音数目却远远不止六个，因为同一个字母在不同条件下可表示不同的音素。如字母 a 单念或无韵尾时读 [A]，在 ai 中读 [a]。

There are only 6 vowels, e.g. a, o, e, i, u and ü in Chinese pronunciation, but the number of vowels in Mandarin is more than that. Because one letter represents different phonemes under different circumstances. For example, the letter a is read [A] when it is read alone or when it has no end of final, but read as [a] in ai.

an 中的 a 读作 [a]，ang 中的 a 读作 [ɑ]；en、eng 中的 e 读作 [ə]；ong 中的 o 读作 [ʊ]。
Letter a is read [a] in an, and [ɑ] in ang; Letter e is read [ə] in en and eng; Letter o is read [ʊ] in ong.

三 汉语普通话声韵母拼合表

Initial-Final Combinations in Chinese Mandarin

声母\韵母	a	o	e	-i [ɿ]	-i [ʅ]	er	ai	ei	ao	ou	an	en	ang	eng	ong
b	ba	bo					bai	bei	bao		ban	ben	bang	beng	
p	pa	po					pai	pei	pao	pou	pan	pen	pang	peng	
m	ma	mo	me				mai	mei	mao	mou	man	men	mang	meng	
f	fa	fo						fei		fou	fan	fen	fang	feng	
d	da		de				dai	dei	dao	dou	dan	den	dang	deng	dong
t	ta		te				tai	tei	tao	tou	tan		tang	teng	tong
n	na		ne				nai	nei	nao	nou	nan	nen	nang	neng	nong
l	la		le				lai	lei	lao	lou	lan		lang	leng	long
z	za		ze	zi			zai	zei	zao	zou	zan	zen	zang	zeng	zong
c	ca		ce	ci			cai		cao	cou	can	cen	cang	ceng	cong
s	sa		se	si			sai		sao	sou	san	sen	sang	seng	song
zh	zha		zhe		zhi		zhai	zhei	zhao	zhou	zhan	zhen	zhang	zheng	zhong
ch	cha		che		chi		chai		chao	chou	chan	chen	chang	cheng	chong
sh	sha		she		shi		shai	shei	shao	shou	shan	shen	shang	sheng	
r			re		ri				rao	rou	ran	ren	rang	reng	rong
j															
q															
x															
g	ga		ge				gai	gei	gao	gou	gan	gen	gang	geng	gong
k	ka		ke				kai	kei	kao	kou	kan	ken	kang	keng	kong
h	ha		he				hai	hei	hao	hou	han	hen	hang	heng	hong

续表

音节声母\韵母	i	ia	iao	ie	iu	ian	in	iang	ing	iong
b	bi		biao	bie		bian	bin		bing	
p	pi		piao	pie		pian	pin		ping	
m	mi		miao	mie	miu	mian	min		ming	
f										
d	di		diao	die	diu	dian			ding	
t	ti		tiao	tie		tian			ting	
n	ni		niao	nie	niu	nian	nin	niang	ning	
l	li	lia	liao	lie	liu	lian	lin	liang	ling	
z										
c										
s										
zh										
ch										
sh										
r										
j	ji	jia	jiao	jie	jiu	jian	jin	jiang	jing	jiong
q	qi	qia	qiao	qie	qiu	qian	qin	qiang	qing	qiong
x	xi	xia	xiao	xie	xiu	xian	xin	xiang	xing	xiong
g										
k										
h										
	yi	ya	yao	ye	you	yan	yin	yang	ying	yong

续表

音节声母\韵母	u	ua	uo	uai	ui	uan	un	uang	ueng	ü	üe	üan	ün
b	bu												
p	pu												
m	mu												
f	fu												
d	du		duo		dui	duan	dun						
t	tu		tuo		tui	tuan	tun						
n	nu		nuo			nuan				nü	nüe		
l	lu		luo			luan	lun			lü	lüe		
z	zu		zuo		zui	zuan	zun						
c	cu		cuo		cui	cuan	cun						
s	su		suo		sui	suan	sun						
zh	zhu	zhua	zhuo	zhuai	zhui	zhuan	zhun	zhuang					
ch	chu	chua	chuo	chuai	chui	chuan	chun	chuang					
sh	shu	shua	shuo	shuai	shui	shuan	shun	shuang					
r	ru	rua	ruo		rui	ruan	run						
j										ju	jue	juan	jun
q										qu	que	quan	qun
x										xu	xue	xuan	xun
g	gu	gua	guo	guai	gui	guan	gun	guang					
k	ku	kua	kuo	kuai	kui	kuan	kun	kuang					
h	hu	hua	huo	huai	hui	huan	hun	huang					
	wu	wa	wo	wai	wei	wan	wen	wang	weng	yu	yue	yuan	yun

第一课 你好

Lesson 1 Hello

声母 Initials

b p m f d t n l g k h

韵母 Finals

a o e i u ü ai ei ao ou

声调 Tones

ˉ(ā) ˊ(á) ˇ(ǎ) ˋ(à)

一 》 生 词 New Words

| 1. | 你 | *pron.* | nǐ | you (single) |
| 2. | 好 | *adj.* | hǎo | good, fine, nice |

本课新字 New Characters

你　好

二 》 课 文 Text

你　好

A：Nǐ hǎo!
　　你 好!

B：Nǐ hǎo!
　　你 好!

三 语音 Phonetics

(一) 声母 Initials

b p m f d t n l g k h

(二) 韵母 Finals

a o e i u ü ai ei ao ou

(三) 声调 Tones

   ˉ   ˊ   ˇ   ˋ

ā　　　　á　　　　ǎ　　　　à

阴平（第一声）　阳平（第二声）　上声（第三声）　去声（第四声）

(四) 音节 Syllables

（b） + a = ba → bā bá bǎ bà
（声母） + 韵母 = 音节

音节 韵母 声母	a	o	e	i	u	ü	ai	ei	ao	ou
b	ba	bo		bi	bu		bai	bei	bao	
p	pa	po		pi	pu		pai	pei	pao	pou
m	ma	mo	me	mi	mu		mai	mei	mao	mou
f	fa	fo			fu			fei		fou
d	da		de	di	du		dai	dei	dao	dou
t	ta		te	ti	tu		tai	tei	tao	tou
n	na		ne	ni	nu	nü	nai	nei	nao	nou
l	la		le	li	lu	lü	lai	lei	lao	lou
g	ga		ge		gu		gai	gei	gao	gou
k	ka		ke		ku		kai	kei	kao	kou
h	ha		he		hu		hai	hei	hao	hou
				yi	wu	yu				

四 注 释 Notes

(一) 汉语的音节 Chinese syllables

1. 汉语音节的构成　Formation of Chinese syllables

汉语的音节大多数由声母、韵母和声调构成。比如 bā（八）、nǐ（你）、dà（大）、kǒu（口）等都是音节。音节开头的辅音叫声母，如 b、n、d、k 等；其余的部分叫韵母，如 a、i、ou 等。韵母共有三类：由一个元音充当的韵母叫单韵母，如 a；由两个或三个元音充当的韵母叫复韵母，如 ai、uai；以后我们还要学习鼻韵母，如 an、ang。

Most Chinese syllables are formed by the combination of the initials, finals and tones, such as bā（八）, nǐ（你）, dà（大）and kǒu（口）. The consonant at the head of a syllable (b, n, d and k in these examples) is called the initials. The rest of the syllables are the finals (a, i and ou). There are three types of finals: A final consists of only one vowel, e.g. a, is called the simple final; a final consists of two or three vowels (ai, uai) is called the compound final; the nasal final, we will study in the future, such as an, ang.

现代汉语普通话系统共 21 个辅音声母，39 个韵母。汉语的音节可能没有开头的辅音声母（零声母），但是一定要有韵母。大部分音节都有声调。如：

There are 21 consonant initials and 39 finals in Chinese Mandarin system. A Chinese syllable may not consist of a consonant initial, but must have a final. Most of the syllables are marked with tones. For example:

成分　　结构 例字	声 母	韵 母	声 调
一 (yī)		i	－ 第一声　1st tone
五 (wǔ)		u	ˇ 第三声　3rd tone
鱼 (yú)		ü	／ 第二声　2nd tone
爱 (ài)		ai	＼ 第四声　4th tone
白 (bái)	b	ai	／ 第二声　2nd tone
飞 (fēi)	f	ei	－ 第一声　1st tone

2. 音节与汉字　Syllables and Chinese characters

在汉语里，通常一个汉字就是一个音节。例如"你"，书写上是一个汉字，也记录了一个音节 nǐ，用于指称第二人称单数。

Usually a Chinese character is a syllable. For example, "你" is a Chinese character, and also is a syllable nǐ, means you, single form.

你 — nǐ — 第二人称单数

有时，同一个音节可以代表很多不同的汉字。例如音节 gē 可以对应不同的汉字，代表不同的意义：

Sometimes, one syllable may represent many different Chinese characters. For example, gē may represent the following four characters:

$$
gē \begin{cases} 戈 & 一种古代兵器 & \text{an ancient weapon} \\ 哥 & 哥哥 & \text{elder brother} \\ 歌 & 歌曲 & \text{song} \\ 割 & 用刀截断 & \text{cut} \end{cases}
$$

所以，虽然汉语有数万个汉字，但是普通话只有 418 个基本音节（如果算上四声和轻声，则有 1,332 个）。

Therefore, there are tens of thousands of characters in Chinese, but only 418 syllables in Mandarin (there are 1,332 if we include the four tones and the neutral tone).

（二）汉语的声调　Tones

1. 声调类别与声调符号　Types and indicators

汉语是有声调的语言。汉语普通话有四个基本声调：阴平、阳平、上声和去声，统称为四声。四声也可以称为第一声、第二声、第三声和第四声。《汉语拼音方案》规定四声用"ˉ、ˊ、ˇ、ˋ"四个符号来表示。声调符号的形状与每个声调高低升降的实际读音有关，如图：

Chinese is a language with tones. There are four basic tones in Chinese Mandarin, which are named high-level tone, rising tone, dipping tone and falling tone. They are called four tones. The four tones can also be called the 1st tone, the 2nd tone, the 3rd tone and the 4th tone. It is regulated in the *Chinese Spelling Programme* that the four tones are indicated by the marks " ˉ , ˊ , ˇ " and " ˋ ". The shapes of four indicators reflect the real pronunciation of syllables, such as high, rising, rising-falling and falling. They can be shown in the following figure:

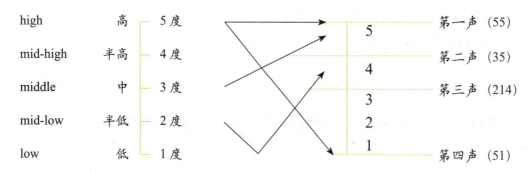

2. 声调与音节的意义　Meanings of tones and syllables

声调在普通话里具有区别意义的重要作用。例如"妈mā"和"马mǎ"两个字，它们的声母和韵母完全一样，区别完全是由声调决定的。

Tones play an important role in distinguishing the meaning in Mandarin. For example, "妈mā" and "马mǎ", they share the same intial and final, but their difference completely depends on the tones.

ma { mā — 妈　mum
     má — 麻　numb
     mǎ — 马　horse
     mà — 骂　scold }

ge { gē — 哥　elder brother
     gé — 格　square
     gě — 舸　barge
     gè — 各　every, each }

（三）三声变调（1）　Modulations of the 3rd tone (1)

汉语中两个第三声音节连读时，前一个要变成第二声。如：

When two 3rd tone syllables are read immediately one after another, the former one is pronounced as the 2nd tone. For example:

nǐ hǎo → ní hǎo　　　wǔbǎi → wúbǎi

（四）音节的书写（1） Writing of syllables (1)

i、u、ü 都可以自成音节。自成音节的时候，分别写成 yi、wu、yu。

i, u and ü may form the independent syllables by themselves. In writing they are respectively yi, wu and yu.

五 》 汉字知识 About Chinese Characters

（一）关于汉字 Chinese characters

汉语的书写符号是汉字。汉字的数量很多，从三千年前甲骨文发展到现在，汉字的总数有五六万个以上。最常用的也有 1,500 个左右。

The written symbols of Chinese language are characters. There are lots of characters in Chinese. Since the invention of the oracle bone scripts more than 3,000 years ago to the present, the total amount of characters is over 50 or 60 thousands. However, only 1,500 of them are most frequently used.

但是汉字是有规律的，它是由一定数量的构件按照一定的规则组合而成。以构件组成的汉字，与音素文字相比，有自己的特点和系统性：

In fact, Chinese characters are regular ones, which are formed by a certain amount of strokes according to certain rules. Comparing with phonemic characters, they have their own characteristics and systematization.

1. 从书写形式上看。音素文字的字母是一个接着一个呈线形展开的，而汉字是方形的，汉字的构件或笔画是以上下、左右、内外等结构形式组合在一个平面方框里。所以也叫方块字。如：

From the view of writing forms, the letters of phonemic characters are linear one after another, while Chinese characters are square, and the strokes of them are combined in a square in the structures such as up-and-down, right-and-left, or inside-and-outside. So they are also called square-block characters. For example：

你 you　　　　马 horse

2. 从数量上看。音素文字的字母数目是有限的，如英文字母只有26个，而汉字的构件数量要多得多，大约有300多个，常用的有100多个。如：

From the view of amount, there are limited letters in the morphy words system. For example, there are only 26 letters in English. There are much more components, about 300 ones, in the system of Chinese characters, among which over 100 strokes are frequently used. For example:

宀：宝　宁　它　守　　　氵：江　河　湖　海
扌：打　扛　抬　提　　　纟：红　级　绸　绞
讠：请　谢　讲　说　　　钅：银　铜　铁　锡
亻：件　作　做　佐　　　口：听　召　问　号
女：好　妈　娘　姑　　　心：思　想　念　急

3. 从造字上看。音素文字中，构成词语的字母与词语的意义之间没有必然的关系，但相当一部分汉字的形、音、义之间原本存在一定的理据。汉字常用的造字方法有四种：

From the view of word-formation, there is no certain meaning connection between the letters forming the word and the word itself in morph-words. However, there are certain connections among the word shape, pronunciation and meaning in many Chinese characters. There are four different types can be identified for Chinese characters:

（1）象形字：描摹所表示的具体事物的形状的独体汉字叫象形字。如下面的"山"字就像一座山的形状。

山（shān mountain）

Pictograms: A single-component character that describes or draws the shape or a certain thing is called the pictogram. For example, the character "山" looks like a mountain.

其他如：Other examples：

火（huǒ fire）　　　　　日（rì sun）　　　　　口（kǒu mouth）

（2）指事字：指事字是由象征性的符号构成或者在象形字的基础上加提示性的符号造出来的独体汉字。如下面的"上"字，古代写作"⌣"，用上面的横来表示"上"的意义。

Ideograms: It is a single-component character formed by adding a direction stroke to an abstract character or to a shape-like one. For example, the following character "上", was written as "⌣" in ancient time, and the short horizontal stroke means "up".

上（shàng up）

其他如：Other examples：

中（zhōng middle）　　　　本（běn booklet）　　　　下（xià down）

(3) 会意字：由两个或两个以上具有意义的偏旁组合在一起表示一个新的意义的汉字叫会意字。如"日"为太阳，"月"表月亮，"日""月"合在一起表示"明亮"的意思。

Semantic compounds: It is formed by combining two or more meaning-representing strokes into a new character with new meaning. For example, "日" indicates the sun and "月" indicates the moon, "日" and "月" combined into a new character "明", which has a new meaning "bright".

明（míng bright）

其他如：Other examples：

炎（yán burning hot）　　森（sēn forest）　　淼（miǎo an expanse water）

(4) 形声字：构成一个字的两个偏旁，一个表示读音、一个表示意义，这种合体字叫形声字。下面一组汉字，左边的偏旁表示意义，如"晴"的左边是"日"，说明这个字的意义跟太阳有关系。这组汉字右边的部分"青"读"qīng"，可以发现，这组汉字的读音都与此相似。

Phono-semantic compounds: It is a multi-component character formed by two radicals, of which one indicates the pronunciation and the other indicates the meaning. Among each of the following characters, the left radical indicates the meaning. For example, the left radical of "晴" is "日", which means that connections exist between the sun and this character. And the right one is "青", which indicates the pronunciation is qīng.

青 (qīng)： 清 (qīng)　　请 (qǐng)　　晴 (qíng)　　情 (qíng)

所以，学习汉字一定要掌握一定量的基本构件和组合规则，这样，可以帮助你更快、更多、更好地记住汉字的字形和字义。

Therefore, it is important to master a certain amount of basic components and the word-formation rules, so as to help you to memorize much more characters quicker and more efficiently.

（二）笔画（1）：基本笔画　Strokes (1) : Basic strokes

汉字的数量虽然很多，但是它们是由一些基本元素构成的，这些基本元素就叫笔画。汉字的笔画有二三十种，这里先介绍其中常用的八种。其他笔画都是由这八种笔画派生出来的。

There are thousands of characters, yet they are formed by some basic components, which are called strokes. There are about 20 or 30 strokes, of which only eight frequently-used ones will be introduced here. Other strokes are all derived by the eight ones.

在书写笔画时，一定要注意笔画的形状和方向，或者从上往下，或者从左往右。这一点非常重要。否则，运笔的方向错了，不但难写、不好看，更严重的是可能错成另一个笔画。

When a character is being written, the shape and direction of the strokes must be noted. It may be from top to bottom, or from left to right. It is very important. Otherwise, if the direction is wrong, the character is hard to write and not beautiful. Sometimes, it even becomes another stroke.

1. 一：（→）　横　héng　horizontal

　　写法：要平，方向从左到右。
　　Rule:　Keep level, write from left to right.
　　例字：一　五　白

2. 丨：（↓）　竖　shù　vertical

　　写法：要直，方向从上到下。
　　Rule:　Keep vertical, write from top to bottom.
　　例字：白　不　口

3. 丿：(丿) 撇 piě throw

　　写法：从右上向左下，呈弧形。注意：如果从左下向右上运笔，就是另一种笔画。

　　Rule: Write from right top to left bottom, like an arc. But if it is written from left bottom to right top, it is another stroke.

　　例字：八　大　你

4. 丶：(㇏) 捺 nà press

　　写法：从左上向右下，呈弧形。

　　Rule: Write from left top to right bottom, like an arc.

　　例字：八　大

5. 丶：(丶) 点 diǎn dot

　　写法：从左上向右下或从右上向左下点，较短。

　　Rule: Write from left top to right bottom, or from right top to left bottom, short.

　　例字：不　爸　然

6. 冫：(㇀) 提 tí upward horizontal

　　写法：笔从左下向右上运动。注意与第三种笔画"丿"的区别。

　　Rule: Write from left bottom to right top, which is different from the 3rd stroke "丿" (throw).

　　例字：打　江　求

7. 乛：(乛) 折 zhé zag
　　乚：(乚)

　　写法："折"可以分成横折（乛）和竖折（乚）两种。注意：这个笔画一定要一笔完成。"乛"先从左向右写横，再拐弯从上向下写竖。"乚"先从上向下写竖，再拐弯从左向右写横。

　　Rule: There are two kinds: horizontal zag (乛) and vertical zag (乚). Pay attention to that it must be written within one stroke. The horizontal zag is written from left to right like a horizontal and turn down to write from top to bottom like a vertical. The vertical zag is written from top to bottom like a vertical, and then turn right and write from left to right like a horizontal.

例字：五 马 口

8. ㇆：（㇆）钩 gōu J hook

写法：笔画到头后转向另一个方向,然后轻快地提起笔带出钩。"钩"可以写成不同的形状。如：

Rule: When a stroke goes to an end, change the direction and then lift the pen forming a hook. There are different shapes of that hook.

    ㇇：横钩（hénggōu   horizontal hook）
    亅：竖钩（shùgōu   vertical hook）
    ㇁：弯钩（wāngōu   clockwise hook）
    ㇂：斜钩（xiégōu   anticlockwise hook）
    ㇉：平钩（pínggōu   level hook）

例字：家 小 打 我 心

（三）怎样避免写错汉字（1）：注意笔画数目
Avoiding writing mistakes (1) : Pay attention to the amount of strokes

每个汉字的笔画数目都是固定的，不能任意增加或减少，多一笔或少一笔就是别的字或者错字，所以写汉字时要特别注意每个字的笔画数目。如：

The stroke amount of every Chinese character is a definite, which cannot be added or reduced. Add or miss one stroke will creat another character or a wrong one. Therefore, one ought to pay special attention to the stroke amount of a character. For example:

人（rén）——大（dà）——太（tài）——犬（quǎn）

少（shǎo）——小（xiǎo）   木（mù）——本（běn）

六 练习 Exercises

(一) 认读声韵母并比较异同　Read and identify the following initials and finals

b—p　　m—f　　d—t　　n—l　　g—k—h

a—o—e　　i—u—ü　　ai—ei　　ao—ou

(二) 声调练习　Tones

yī — yí — yǐ — yì　　　　wū — wú — wǔ — wù

yū — yú — yǔ — yù　　　　mī — mí — mǐ — mì

fū — fú — fǔ — fù　　　　gē — gé — gě — gè

bō — bó — bǒ — bò　　　　nā — ná — nǎ — nà

pāi — pái — pǎi — pài　　　fēi — féi — fěi — fèi

dāo — dáo — dǎo — dào　　hōu — hóu — hǒu — hòu

(三) 朗读音节，注意声母的区别　Read the syllables and identify the initials' differences

bā—pā　　dā—tā　　nā—lā　　mā—fā

bō—pō　　dì—tì　　nǚ—lǚ　　méi—féi

(四) 认读音节　Read and learn the syllables

kǒu　yī　nǐ　hǎo　dà　bái　wǔ　bā　mǎ　bù

wú　dào　gǒu　lǚ　tǎ　tì　fá　měi　dú　tái

nǐ hǎo　wǔbǎi　dà mǎ　dà kǒu　bái mǎ　pá pō　měidé

(五) 变调练习　Modulations of tones

yǔfǎ　bǐnǐ　pǎo mǎ　mǎpǐ　fǔdǎo　fǔdǐ

dǎ bǎ　tǎohǎo　gǔyǔ　kǎitǐ　kǎogǔ　kǒuyǔ

(六) 将下列韵母写成音节　Change the following finals into syllables

i → _____　　　　u → _____　　　　ü → _____

(七) 汉字练习　Writing Chinese characters

1. 描写笔画　Trace the following strokes

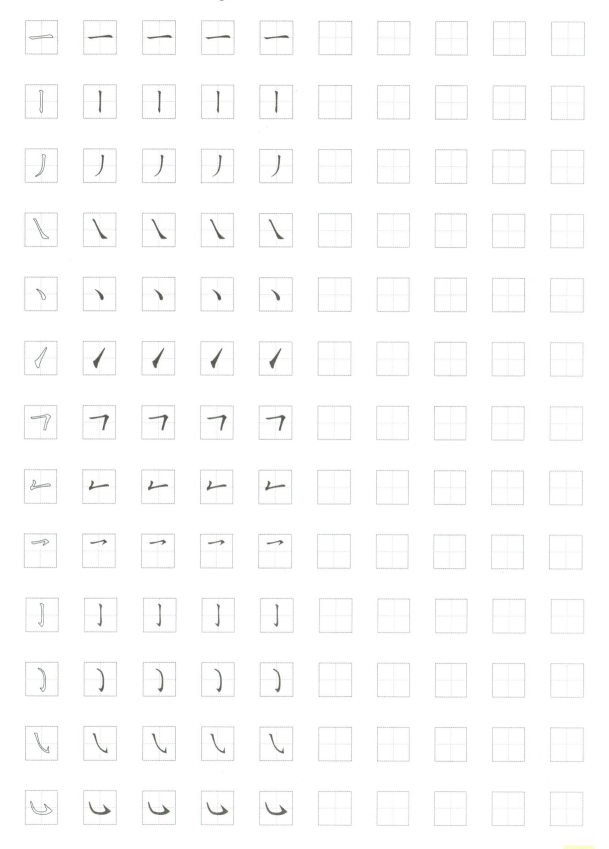

2. 描写汉字 Trace the following characters

| 你 | 丿 | 亻 | 亻 | 伫 | 伱 | 你 | | |
| 好 | ㄑ | 乆 | 女 | 奵 | 奵 | 好 | | |

3. 临写本课笔画并比较异同 Copy the strokes of this lesson and pay attention to their differences and similarities

一: _____   丨: _____

丿: _____   丶: _____

、: _____   ㇀: _____

𠃍: _____   ㇄: _____

4. 写出包括下列笔画的汉字（选做）Write some Chinese characters with the following strokes (optional work)

一: _____   丨: _____

丿: _____   丶: _____

、: _____   ㇀: _____

𠃍: _____   ㇄: _____

文化小贴士 Proverb

Hǎohǎo xuéxí, tiāntiān xiàng shàng!
好好学习，天天向上！

Study hard and make progress every day !

第二课
汉语难吗

Lesson 2
Is Chinese difficult

韵母 Finals

an　　en　　ang　　eng　　ong

一 >> 生 词 New Words

1.	吗	*particle*	ma	used at the end of a question
2.	很	*adv.*	hěn	very, quite
3.	忙	*adj.*	máng	busy
4.	汉语	*n.*	Hànyǔ	Chinese language, Chinese
5.	难	*adj.*	nán	difficult, hard
6.	不	*adv.*	bù	not
7.	太	*adv.*	tài	excessively, too, over

33

本课新字 New Characters

| 吗 | 很 | 忙 | 汉 | 语 | 难 | 不 | 太 |

二 课文 Text

汉语难吗

A: Nǐ hǎo ma?
你好吗?

B: Hěn hǎo.
很好。

A: Nǐ máng ma?
你忙吗?

B: Hěn máng.
很忙。

A: Hànyǔ nán ma?
汉语难吗?

B: Hànyǔ bú tài nán.
汉语不太难。

汉语难吗?
汉语不太难。

三 语 音 Phonetics

（一）韵母 Finals

an　en　ang　eng　ong

（二）拼音 Pinyin

音节 声母 \ 韵母	an	en	ang	eng	ong
b	ban	ben	bang	beng	
p	pan	pen	pang	peng	
m	man	men	mang	meng	
f	fan	fen	fang	feng	
d	dan	den	dang	deng	dong
t	tan		tang	teng	tong
n	nan	nen	nang	neng	nong
l	lan		lang	leng	long
g	gan	gen	gang	geng	gong
k	kan	ken	kang	keng	kong
h	han	hen	hang	heng	hong

四 注 释 Notes

（一）声调的标写（1） Writing of tones (1)

声调要标写在音节的主要元音上。

A tone-indicator is placed above a main vowel of a syllable.

1. 只有一个元音韵母时，声调标在这个元音上。如：

A tone-indicator is placed above the vowel if it is a single-final. For example:

dà　pò　tē　mǐ　bǔ　lù

2. 韵母由两个或两个以上的元音构成时，声调一般按照 a、o、e、i、u、ü 的顺序标写，前一个韵母优先。但韵母中 i、u 都有时，则要标在后一韵母上，这一点我们以后再详细学。如：

When a final consists of two or more vowels, the tone-indicator is generally placed above the vowels in the order of a, o, e, i, u and ü, and the former vowel is preferred. However, if both i and u in a final, it must be put on the later. We will study it in detail later. For example:

  dāi dēi dāo dōu diū

3. 声调符号如果需要标在 i 上，那么 i 上的小点要省掉。如：

If a tone-indicator is placed above i, the dot on the top of i must be omitted. For example:

  bǐyì cíyì

（二）轻声　The neutral tone

汉语中有些音节不带声调，这样的音节叫轻声。读的时候，轻声音节读得很轻、很短。在书写时，轻声音节不标声调。例如：

Some syllables in Chinese are toneless. They are called neutral tones and pronounced light and short. Do not carry any tone-indicators in writing a neutral tone. For example:

  māma yīfu dōngxi wǒmen bái de

（三）"不"的变调　Modulations of "不"

1. "不"的本调是第四声，但是在另一个第四声音节前面时，应该读成第二声。如：
The basic tone for "不" is the 4th tone. It changes into the 2nd tone when it is immediately followed by another 4th tone syllable. For example:

  búbì búcè búdàn búdàng búcuò búgòu
  búgù búdìng búlài búlì búguò búyì

2. 夹在词语中间时读轻声。如：
It must be read with a neutral tone when it is between two words. For example:

  máng bu máng lěng bu lěng kǔ bu kǔ gòu bu gòu

五 汉字知识 About Chinese Characters

（一）汉字的结构（1） Structures of Chinese characters (1)

从结构上来说，汉字可分两种：一种是独体字，独体字在结构上是由一个部件构成的，不能切分。如：

Considering the structure, there are two kinds of Chinese characters. One is single-component characters, which is formed by only component and cannot be divided again. For example:

另一种是合体字。汉字大多数是合体字，如"你""好"等。合体字是由几个部件组合而成的，有三种基本的结构方式：上下结构、左右结构和包围结构。

Another one is multi-component characters. Most characters in Chinese are multi-components ones, such as "你" and "好". A multi-component character consists of several components. The three basic structures are up-and-down structure, left-and-right structure and enclosed structure.

上下结构　up-and-down structure：　爸　哥　弟

左右结构　left-and-right structure：　汉　语　好

包围结构　enclosed structure：　　　国　有　习　这

（二）笔画（2）：派生笔画 Strokes (2): Derivative strokes

派生笔画是由基本笔画组合或稍加变形组合而成的。要注意，所有派生笔画都只是一个笔画，要一笔写成。

Derivative strokes consist of basic strokes or slightly changed basic strokes. Pay attention to that all the derivative strokes are single strokes, which must be written by one stroke.

1. ㇇：（㇇）　　撇点　　piědiǎn　throw-dot

　　　　　　　　注意：　撇不要太长，拐弯后的点要长一点儿。

　　　　　　　　Rules:　The throw stroke cannot be too long, but the dot ought to be longer after the turning.

　　　　　　　　例字：　好　她

2. ㄅ：（㇆） 横折钩 héngzhégōu horizontal-zag-J hook
   例字：也 她

3. ㄴ：（乚） 竖弯钩 shùwāngōu vertical-anticlockwise curve-J hook
   例字：也 他

4. ㄅ：（㇗） 竖折折钩 shùzhézhégōu vertical-zag-zag-J hook
   例字：马 弟

5. ㄱ：（㇇） 横撇 héngpiě horizontal-throw
   例字：又 难

（三）笔画关系 Stroke relations

一个汉字中的笔画之间总的来说存在三种关系：相离、相接、相交。

Generally speaking, there are three relations among strokes, and they are separated, connected and intersected relations.

相离：两个笔画之间不直接接触。如：八、分。

Separated: No direct connections exist between two strokes. For example: 八，分．

相接：两个笔画之间接触，但不相交。如：人、入。

Connected: Direct connections exist between two strokes. For example: 人，入．

相交：两个笔画之间相交叉。如：十、大。

Intersected: Two strokes intersect each other. For example: 十，大．

笔画间的关系非常重要，如果关系搞错了，那么这个字就是一个错字，或者变成了一个别的字。如"五"，第一笔的横和第二笔的竖是相接关系，如果变成相离或相交关系，变成"五""五"，那么就成了错字。又如，"上午""下午"的"午（wǔ）"字，其中的第二笔横和第四笔竖是相接关系，如果变成相交关系，那么就成了另一个汉字"牛（niú）"。"己（jǐ）""已（yǐ）""巳（sì）"也是因为笔画间关系的不同而成为三个不同汉字的。所以，要写好、写对汉字一定要注意笔画之间的关系。

Stroke relations are quite important. If they are mistaken, the Chinese character will be a wrong one or become another one. Take "五" for example, the 2nd stroke connects to the 1st stroke, if they are departed or intersected, it becomes "五" and "五", which are wrong characters. Take "午（wǔ）" for another example, in which the 2nd stroke and the 4th one is connected relation. If it is changed into intersected one, it become another character "牛 (niú)". And "己 (jǐ)" "已 (yǐ)" and "巳 (sì)" are different characters because of the different stroke relations. Therefore, in order to write Chinese characters well and correctly, we must pay attention to the relationship between strokes.

（四）笔顺（1）：先上后下，先左后右
Stroke orders (1): From top to bottom, from left to right

在书写一个汉字时，有的笔画要先写，有的要后写，笔画之间具有一定的顺序，这就是笔顺。如"八"字，应该先写撇再写捺。记住笔顺可以帮助你更快、更好地书写汉字。从本课开始，我们将逐步介绍汉字的笔顺规则。

When write a Chinese character, some strokes ought to be written first, and some later. There is a certain order among the strokes, which is called stroke orders. For instance, in writing "八", the throw stroke is written first and the press one the second. Memorizing stroke orders may help you to write a Chinese character beautifully and quickly. From this lesson, we will gradually introduce the stroke-order rules of Chinese characters.

规则一：先上后下　　Rule 1: From top to bottom

汉字的笔画一般是从上往下写的；构件之间也按照从上到下的顺序，先写上边的，再写下边的。如：

Normally, a Chinese character is written from top to bottom, so is a component. The upper strokes or components are written first, and then the lower ones. For example:

五：一 丁 五 五　　　　　　　　不：一 丆 不 不

爸：丿 八 ハ 父 父 爷 爷 爸

哥：一 ㄱ ㄲ 可 可 퍔 픞 픞 哥

规则二：先左后右　　Rule 2: From left to right

写汉字时，应该按照从左到右的顺序，先写左边的笔画或构件，再写右边的。如：
A Chinese character is written from left to right. That is, the left strokes or components are written first, then the right ones. For example:

八：丿 八　　　　　　　　汉：丶 冫 氵 汉 汉

语：丶 讠 讠 订 评 评 语 语　　好：乀 乂 女 女 好 好

（五）怎样避免写错汉字（2）：注意笔画形状
Avoiding writing mistakes (2) : Pay attention to the shape of strokes

每个汉字每个笔画的形状都是固定的，如果改变了笔画的形状，就会成为别的字或错字。所以，写汉字的时候，要注意每个笔画的形状。如：

The stroke shape in every Chinese character is fixed. If it is changed, the character will become another one or a wrong one. Therefore, one should pay close attention to the stroke shapes. For example:

贝（bèi　最后一笔为点　　Last stroke is a dot.）

见（jiàn　最后一笔为竖弯钩　Last stroke is vertical-anticlockwise curve-J hook.）

换（huàn　最后一笔为捺　　Last stroke is press.）

挽（wǎn　最后一笔为竖弯钩　Last stroke is vertical-anticlockwise curve-J hook.）

风（fēng　第三笔为撇　　The 3rd stroke is throw.）

凤（fèng　第三笔为横撇　　The 3rd stroke is horizontal-throw.）

六　练习　Exercises

（一）认读韵母并比较异同　Learn and identify the following finals

an — ang　　　　en — eng　　　　ang — eng — ong

（二）声调练习　Tones

bā — bá — bǎ — bà　　　　gā — gá — gǎ — gà
dī — dí — dǐ — dì　　　　tāi — tái — tǎi — tài
hōng — hóng — hǒng — hòng　　　nān — nán — nǎn — nàn
mēng — méng — měng — mèng　　　pū — pú — pǔ — pù

（三）认读音节并比较异同　Learn and identify the following syllables

bàngōng — bānggōng　　fǎngǎn — fǎn gōng　　tānlán — tángláng
dāndāng — dāngbān　　fēifán — fēifèn　　　　fēndān — fēn hóng
téngtòng — téngkōng　　fēnfāng — fēngfān　　nónggēng — lǒngtǒng

（四）轻声变调　The neutral tone and modulations

1. 轻声　The neutral tone

bàba　　　māma　　　gēge　　　dìdi　　　mèimei　　　mōmo　　　kànkan　　　lái ba

nǐ ne　　　tā de　　　lìhai　　　dǎban　　　wūli　　　mùtou　　　wǔ ge　　　pǎo le

2. "不"的变调　Modulation of "不"

búbì　　　bú bàn　　　bú dà　　　búdài　　　búdàn　　　búgù

búgòu　　　búbiàn　　　búdàng　　　búlài　　　búlì　　　búduàn

là bu là　　　dà bu dà　　　kǔ bu kǔ　　　máng bu máng　　　lěng bu lěng

（五）认读并连线　Read, learn and match

吗	hàn	你	nán
很	yǔ	好	nǐ
汉	hěn	太	hǎo
语	ma	难	tài

（六）请给下列音节标上声调　Indicate the tones on the following syllables

第四声 丶：ba → ___　　po → ___　　te → ___　　mi → ___　　du → ___　　lu → ___

第三声 ˇ：bi → ___　　pi → ___　　di → ___　　ti → ___　　li → ___　　yi → ___

第二声 ´：bai → ___　　mei → ___　　tao → ___　　lou → ___　　li → ___　　lu → ___

（七）汉字练习　Writing Chinese characters

1. 描写笔画　Trace the following strokes

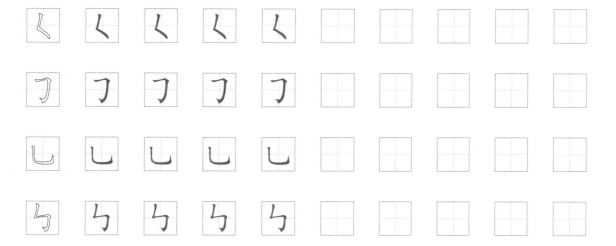

㇇ ㇇ ㇇ ㇇ ㇇

2．描写汉字　Trace the following characters

吗 … 吗 吗

很 … 很

忙 … 忙 忙

汉 丶 冫 氵 汈 汉

语 … 语

太 一 ナ 大 太

难 … 难

难

3．临写本课笔画并注意笔画间的异同　Copy the strokes of this lesson and pay attention to their differences and similarities

㇛：____________________　　㇆：____________________

㇄：____________________　　㇌：____________________

㇇：____________________

4. 根据笔画间的关系对下列汉字归类　Sort the following characters on their structures

　　　　　　　八　工　人　入　大　小　土　斤

相离　Separated：_____

相接　Connected：_____

相交　Intersected：_____

5. 写出下列汉字的笔画数　Write out the amount of strokes of following characters

吗（ ）　很（ ）　你（ ）　好（ ）　难（ ）　汉（ ）

6. 写出包括下列笔画的汉字（选做）Write out some Chinese characters with the following strokes (optional work)

乀：_____　　　丁：_____

乚：_____　　　㇀：_____

刁：_____

文化小贴士　Proverb

Shūshān yǒu lù qín wéi jìng, xuéhǎi wú yá kǔ zuò zhōu.
书山有路勤为径，学海无涯苦作舟。

Diligence is the path to the mountain of knowledge,
hard-working is the boat to the endless sea of learning.

第三课 今天星期几

Lesson 3 What day is it today

声母 Initials

j q x

韵母 Finals

(i-)	ia	ie	iao	iou (iu)
	ian	in	iang	ing	iong
(ü-)	üe	üan	ün		

一 生词 New Words

1.	请	v.	qǐng	please
2.	进	v.	jìn	enter, come in, go into
3.	的	particle	de	of, used after an attributive word or phrase

4.	书	n.	shū	book
5.	谢谢	v.	xièxie	thanks
6.	客气	v.	kèqi	polite, courteous, modest
7.	今天	n.	jīntiān	today
8.	星期	n.	xīngqī	week
	星期一	n.	xīngqīyī	Monday
	星期二	n.	xīngqī'èr	Tuesday
	星期三	n.	xīngqīsān	Wednesday
	星期四	n.	xīngqīsì	Thursday
	星期五	n.	xīngqīwǔ	Friday
	星期六	n.	xīngqīliù	Saturday
	星期天	n.	xīngqītiān	Sunday
9.	几	pron.	jǐ	how many, how much
10.	有	v.	yǒu	have, possess
11.	课	n.	kè	subject, course
12.	英语	n.	Yīngyǔ	English (language)

本课新字 New Characters

请 进 的 书 谢 客 气 今

天 星 期 几 有 课 英 语

二 课文 Texts

（一）请 进

（在宿舍）

A：请进！
Qǐng jìn!

B：你的书。
Nǐ de shū.

A：谢谢！
Xièxie!

B：不客气！
Bú kèqi!

（二）今天星期几

（在家里）

A：今天 星期 几？
Jīntiān xīngqī jǐ?

B：今天 星期一。
Jīntiān xīngqīyī.

A：你有课吗？
Nǐ yǒu kè ma?

B：有，有英语课。
Yǒu, yǒu Yīngyǔkè.

今天星期几？

今天星期一。

三 》 语 音 Phonetics

（一）声母 Initials

j　　q　　x

（二）韵母 Finals

(i-)	ia	ie	iao	iou (iu)
	ian	in	iang	ing	iong
(ü-)	üe	üan	ün

（三）拼音 Pinyin

音节 声母 \ 韵母	i	ia	ie	iao	iou	ian	in	iang	ing	iong
j	ji	jia	jie	jiao	jiu	jian	jin	jiang	jing	jiong
q	qi	qia	qie	qiao	qiu	qian	qin	qiang	qing	qiong
x	xi	xia	xie	xiao	xiu	xian	xin	xiang	xing	xiong
b	bi		bie	biao		bian	bin		bing	
p	pi		pie	piao		pian	pin		ping	
m	mi		mie	miao		mian	min		ming	
d	di		die	diao	diu	dian			ding	
t	ti		tie	tiao		tian			ting	
n	ni		nie	niao	niu	nian	nin	niang	ning	
l	li	lia	lie	liao	liu	lian	lin	liang	ling	
		ya	ye	yao	you	yan	yin	yang	ying	yong

音节 韵母 声母	ü	üe	üan	ün
n	nü	nüe		
l	lü	lüe		
j	ju	jue	juan	jun
q	qu	que	quan	qun
x	xu	xue	xuan	xun
	yu	yue	yuan	yun

四 注 释 Notes

（一）三声变调（2） Modulation of 3rd tones (2)

第三声音节位于一个第一声、第二声、第四声或轻声音节前面时，这个三声音节要读成半三声。也就是说，只读第三声的前半下降部分，不读后面上升的部分，接着马上读下面的音节。如：

The 3rd tone syllable becomes a half 3rd tone when it is immediately followed by a 1st, 2nd, 4th or neutral tone syllable. That is, only the first half falling part of the tone is pronounced, while the rising part following is not pronounced, and is immediately followed by the next syllable. For example:

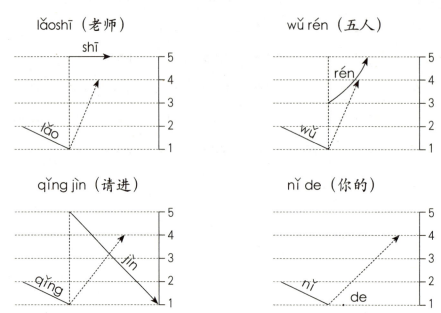

（二）音节的书写（2） Writing of syllables (2)

以 i、ü 做韵头的音节书写时要注意：
Pay attention to the syllables headed by i, ü in writing:

1. 以 i 开头的韵母　Finals headed by i

(1) i、in、ing 自成音节时，需在前面加上 y。如：
When i, in, ing form a syllable by themselves, y is added in front of i, in, ing. For example:

　　i → yi　　　in → yin　　　ing → ying

(2) 其他以 i 开头的韵母自成音节时，将 i 改成 y。如：
When the other finals headed by i is used as a syllable, it is changed into y. For example:

　　ia → ya　　　　　ie → ye　　　　　iao → yao　　　　　iou → you
　　ian → yan　　　　iang → yang　　　iong → yong

2. 以 ü 开头的韵母　Finals headed by ü

(1) 自成音节时，在前面加上 y，ü 上两点省略。如：
When ü forms a syllable by itself, y is added in front of ü, and the two dots on ü must be omitted. For example:

　　üe → yue　　　üan → yuan　　　ün → yun

(2) 跟声母 j、q、x 拼的时候，写成 ju、qu、xu 等，ü 上两点省略，这是因为 u 及以 u 开头的韵母不能和声母 j、q、x 拼合。
When ü is combined with initials of j, q and x, they are written into ju, qu and xu, of which the dots on ü must be omitted, because u and the finals headed by u cannot be combined with initials of j, q and x.

(3) 跟声母 n、l 相拼的时候，ü 上两点不能省略，仍然写成 nü、lü 等，这是因为 u 及以 u 开头的韵母也能和声母 n、l 拼合。
When ü is combined with initials of n and l, they are written into nü and lü, of which the dots on ü cannot be omitted, because u and the finals headed by u can also be combined with initials of n and l.

五 汉字知识 About Chinese Characters

(一) 汉字的结构 (2) Structures of Chinese characters (2)

汉字的基本结构是上下结构、左右结构和包围结构。这三种结构每一种内部又有不同的结构方式。

Top-bottom structure, left-right structure and enclosed structure are the basic structures of Chinese characters. There are different types of structures among the three basic structures.

上下结构 Top-bottom structure

上下相等	Top equals bottom	⊟	爸 哥
上小下大	Small top and big bottom	⊟	英 弟
上大下小	Big top and small bottom	⊟	怎 点

左右结构 Left-right structure

左右相等	Left equals right	⊞	好 的
左小右大	Small left and big right	⊞	汉 语
左大右小	Big left and small right	⊞	那 划

包围结构 Enclosed structure

(1) 全包围　Fully-enclosed structure　□　回 国

(2) 半包围　Half-enclosed structure

　　左上包围　Left-top enclosed　⌐　有 店

右上包围	Right-top enclosed	⌐	习 句
左下包围	Left bottom enclosed	∟	进 这
左上右包围	Left-top-right enclosed	⊓	同 风
左下右包围	Left-bottom-right enclosed	⊔	画 凶

（二）笔画（3）：派生笔画　Strokes (3) : Derivative stokes

1. ㇇：（㇇） 横折折撇　héngzhézhépiě　horizontal-zag-zag-throw
   例字：进　这　建

2. ㇊：（㇊） 横折提　héngzhétí　horizontal-zag-upward horizontal
   例字：语　请

3. 乙：（乙） 横折弯钩（1）héngzhéwāngōu　horizontal-zag-anticlockwise
   例字：九　几　　　　　curve-J hook

4. ㇈：（㇈） 撇折　piězhé　throw-zag
   例字：法　么

（三）笔顺（2）：先横后竖，先撇后捺

Stroke orders (2) : Horizontal before vertical; diagonals right-to-left before diagonals left-to-right

规则三：先横后竖　Rule 3: Horizontal before vertical

横和由横派生的笔画跟竖、撇、捺等相交叉时，应该先写横类笔画，再写其他笔画。如：

When a horizontal stroke or its derivatives intersects with a vertical, throw or press stroke, the horizontal stroke is written first and then the rest. For example：

十：一　十　　　　七：一　七　　　　力：乛　力

注意："先横后竖"是一个一般原则，有些情况例外。

Note: "Horizontal before vertical" is a general principle. Sometime, it also has exceptions.

当"先横后竖"的原则和"先左后右"矛盾时，往往"先左后右"原则优先，先写左边的其他笔画，再写右边的横类笔画。这时，横和其他笔画的关系往往不是相交关系，而是相接等关系。如：

When "Horizontal before vertical" and "left before right" conflicts, usually the later has the priority. The left strokes are written first, then the horizontal strokes on the right. In this case, the horizontal stroke does not intersect with other strokes, but connects to them. For example:

口：丨 冂 口   几：丿 几

另外，为了字的整体平衡，有些情况横也要后写。当横在竖的一侧时，要先写竖。如：

Sometimes, to keep balance, horizontal strokes should be written later. When a horizontal stroke is on the side of a vertical stroke, the vertical stroke is written first. For example：

上：丨 卜 上   北：丨 ᅥ ォ ォ 北

有些字横在中间，而且地位突出，横也要后写。如：

In some characters, the horizontal stroke is in the middle and outstanding, then, it cannot be written first. For example：

子：ㄱ 了 子   女：く 女 女

规则四：先撇后捺   Rule 4: Diagonals right-to-left before diagonals left-to-right

撇和捺在一起时，一般先写撇或由撇组合成的笔画，再写捺。如：

When a throw stroke is written together with a press one, usually, the throw stroke or its combinations should be written before the press stroke. For example：

人：丿 人   又：フ 又

（四）怎样避免写错汉字（3）：注意笔画长短
Avoiding writing mistakes (3) : Pay attention to the length of strokes

有些汉字中，笔画的长短也是固定的，如果违反了笔画之间的长短关系，就可能成为错字或别的汉字。所以，写汉字时还要注意笔画的长短。如：

In some characters, the length of strokes is fixed, if it is not taken into serious consideration, the character will become other characters, or a wrong one. For example：

二 (èr) → 二 (×)　　　　工 (gōng) → 工 (×)

土 (tǔ) → 士 (shì)　　　　未 (wèi) → 末 (mò)

六 练 习　Exercises

（一）认读声韵母并比较异同　Read and identify the following initials and finals

j　　q　　x　　　iang　　　ing　　　iong

i—ü　　ie—üe　　ian—uan　　in—ün　　ia—iao—iu

（二）声调练习　Tones

jī — jí — jǐ — jì　　　　jū — jú — jǔ — jù
jiē — jié — jiě — jiè　　　　jiā — jiá — jiǎ — jià
qī — qí — qǐ — qì　　　　qīng — qíng — qǐng — qìng
quān — quán — quǎn — quàn　　　　xiāng — xiáng — xiǎng — xiàng
xīn — xín — xǐn — xìn　　　　xiān — xián — xiǎn — xiàn

（三）认读音节并比较异同　Read and identify the following syllables

juéjì—jiājù　　　　jīxiè—jíqiè　　　　quēxí—quánjí

qíjǐng—qíjiàn　　　　quánjú—xuánjī　　　　quán jiā—jiàqian

júxiàn—jīxiè　　　　xiànqī—xiángxì　　　　qióngjìn—qiánjìn

jījiàn—qìqiāng　　　　xiàjiā—xiàngyá　　　　jiānqiáng—xiànxiàng

53

（四）变调　Modulations of tones

běibian　fǎngē　huǒguō　xǔduō　dǎjī　lǎocū　qiántān
bǎncái　měidé　dàtóu　lǚxíng　lǎonián　jiǎngtái　hǎopíng
kěnqiè　lǎoliàn　hǎiyàn　gǎnxiè　lǎotài　wǎnhuì　tiělù
wǔ ge　wǒ de　xiǎojiě　lǎohǔ

（五）认读并连线　Read, learn and match

请	jǐ		有	qī
天	jìn		书	yīng
进	kè		期	xīng
谢	jīn		语	yǔ
客	tiān		不	bù
今	xiè		星	shū
几	qǐng		英	yǒu

（六）写音节　Syllables writing

in → _____　　ing → _____　　ia → _____　　ie → _____

iao → _____　　iou → _____　　ian → _____　　iong → _____

üe → _____　　üan → _____　　ün → _____

j + ü (ˉ) → _____　　　x + ü (ˉ) → _____

n + ü (ˇ) → _____　　　l + ü (ˋ) → _____

（七）汉字练习　Writing Chinese characters

1. 描写笔画　Trace the following strokes

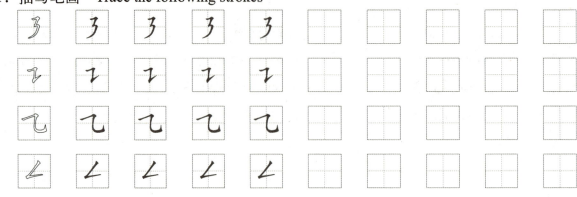

2. 描写汉字 Trace the following characters

课

英 一 十 艹 艹 艹 艹 英 英

3. 写出下列汉字的笔画数　Write out the amount of strokes of the following characters

请（　）　进（　）　谢（　）　客（　）　期（　）

4. 写出包括下列笔画的汉字（选做）　Write some Chinese characters including the following strokes (optional)

亅：_____　乛：_____

乙：_____　乚：_____

5. 写出下列汉字的笔顺　Write out the stroke orders of the following characters

十：_____　今：_____

几：_____　天：_____

书：_____

6. 写出十个左右结构的汉字　Write out about ten characters with left-right structure

7. 临写本课笔画、汉字并比较与以前所学笔画间的异同　Copy the strokes and characters learnt in this lesson, and compare with those learnt before

文化小贴士　Proverb

Yí cùn guāngyīn yí cùn jīn, cùn jīn nán mǎi cùn guāngyīn.
一寸光阴一寸金，寸金难买寸光阴。

An inch of time is an inch of gold,
and an inch of gold cannot afford an inch of time.

第四课
这是什么

Lesson 4
What is this

声母 Initials

z　　c　　s　　zh　　ch　　sh　　r

韵母 Finals

-i [ɿ]　　　-i [ʅ]　　　er
(u-)　　ua　　　uo　　　uai　　　uei (ui)
　　　　uan　　uen (un)　uang　　ueng

一 》 生词 New Words

1.	这	*pron.*	zhè	this
2.	是	*v.*	shì	be
3.	什么	*pron.*	shénme	what

57

4.	词典	n.	cídiǎn	dictionary
5.	早上	n.	zǎoshang	morning, early morning
6.	去	v.	qù	go
7.	食堂	n.	shítáng	canteen, dining room
8.	我	pron.	wǒ	I, me
9.	回	v.	huí	return, go back
10.	宿舍	n.	sùshè	dormitory
11.	哪儿	pron.	nǎr	where
12.	教室	n.	jiàoshì	classroom
13.	再见	v.	zàijiàn	goodbye

本课新字 New Characters

这 是 什 么 词 典 早
上 去 食 堂 我 回 宿
舍 哪 儿 教 室 再 见

二 课文 Texts

（一）这是什么

A：你好！
Nǐ hǎo!

B：你好！
Nǐ hǎo!

A：这是什么？
Zhè shì shénme?

B：这是汉语词典。
Zhè shì Hànyǔ cídiǎn.

（二）你去食堂吗

A：Zǎoshang hǎo！
早上 好！

B：Zǎoshang hǎo！
早上 好！

A：Nǐ qù shítáng ma？
你去食堂吗？

B：Bù，wǒ huí sùshè。Nǐ qù nǎr？
不，我回宿舍。你去哪儿？

A：Wǒ qù jiàoshì。
我去教室。

B：Zàijiàn！
再见！

A：Zàijiàn！
再见！

三 语 音 Phonetics

（一）声母 Initials

z c s zh ch sh r

（二）韵母 Finals

-i [ɿ]　　-i [ʅ]　　er
(u-)　　ua　　uo　　uai　　uei (ui)
　　　　uan　　uen (un)　　uang　　ueng

(三) 拼音 *Pinyin*

声母\音节\韵母	a	e	-i	ai	ei	ao	ou	an	en	ang	eng	ong
z	za	ze	zi	zai	zei	zao	zou	zan	zen	zang	zeng	zong
c	ca	ce	ci	cai	cei	cao	cou	can	cen	cang	ceng	cong
s	sa	se	si	sai		sao	sou	san	sen	sang	seng	song
zh	zha	zhe	zhi	zhai	zhei	zhao	zhou	zhan	zhen	zhang	zheng	zhong
ch	cha	che	chi	chai		chao	chou	chan	chen	chang	cheng	chong
sh	sha	she	shi	shai	shei	shao	shou	shan	shen	shang	sheng	
r		re	ri			rao	rou	ran	ren	rang	reng	rong

声母\音节\韵母	u	ua	uo	uai	uei (ui)	uan	uen (un)	uang	ueng
d	du		duo		dui	duan	dun		
t	tu		tuo		tui	tuan	tun		
n	nu		nuo			nuan			
l	lu		luo			luan	lun		
g	gu	gua	guo	guai	gui	guan	gun	guang	
k	ku	kua	kuo	kuai	kui	kuan	kun	kuang	
h	hu	hua	huo	huai	hui	huan	hun	huang	
z	zu		zuo		zui	zuan	zun		
c	cu		cuo		cui	cuan	cun		
s	su		suo		sui	suan	sun		
zh	zhu	zhua	zhuo	zhuai	zhui	zhuan	zhun	zhuang	
ch	chu	chua	chuo	chuai	chui	chuan	chun	chuang	
sh	shu	shua	shuo	shuai	shui	shuan	shun	shuang	
r	ru	rua	ruo		rui	ruan	run		
		wa	wo	wai	wei	wan	wen	wang	weng

四 注释 Notes

(一) er 和儿化韵　　er and the retroflex finals

1. er 是普通话里一个特殊的元音韵母，汉语拼音用两个字母表示，实际上只是一个元音。er 是一个卷舌韵母，它只能自成音节。如：

er is a special vowel final in Mandarin. It is signed by two letters in *pinyin*, which is actually regarded as one vowel. er is a retroflex final, which can only form a syllable itself. For example:

érqiě　而且　　　　ěrjī　耳机

2．er 的作用主要是和别的韵母结合成一个"儿化韵"。韵母儿化时，本身要发生一些细微的变化。儿化韵的写法是在原来的韵母后面加上 r，汉字的写法是在原来的汉字后加一个"儿"字。如：

The main role of er is to form a retroflex syllable in combination with other finals. When a final is retroflexed, it changes slightly. In transcription, it is shown by adding r to the original form. In written language it is represented by"儿". For example:

花儿　huār　　　　小孩儿　xiǎohái r

注意：这里 r 是用以表示卷舌的符号，不等于辅音 r。

Note:　r here is a symbol of retroflex. It is not the consonant r.

(二) 隔音符号　　Dividing mark

隔音符号用（'）表示，它的作用是用来分清音节之间的界限。以 a、o、e 开头的音节跟在其他音节后面时，如果音节之间的界限不清楚，连写的多音节词有可能引起歧义，那么需用隔音符号（'）隔开。如：

Dividing mark is represented by the symbol ('), which is used to divide the syllables. When syllables headed by a, o or e follows another syllable, misunderstanding takes place if there is no clear dividing mark between them. So it is desirable to use a dividing mark (') to clarity the boundary between the two syllables so as to avoid the misunderstanding. For example:

pí'ǎo → 皮袄　　　　(piào → 票)

（三）音节的书写（3） Writing of syllables (3)

1. 以 u 为韵头的韵母自成音节时，需将 u 改成 w。如：

When a final headed by u forms a syllable itself, u should be changed into w. For example：

ua → wa	（蛙）	uo → wo	（窝）
uai → wai	（歪）	uei → wei	（威）
uan → wan	（弯）	uen → wen	（温）
uang → wang	（汪）	ueng → weng	（翁）

2. 韵母 iou、uei、uen 前面有声母时必须省写成 iu、ui、un。如：

When iou, uei or uen follows an initial, they must be written as iu, ui or un. For example：

l + iou → liu　　d + uei → dui　　t + uen → tun

（四）声调的标写（2） Tone marks (2)

一个音节中如果 i 和 u 同时出现，那么，声调标在后一个元音上。如：

If i and u exist in the same syllable, the second vowel takes the tone mark. For example:

liú　　duì

五　汉字知识 About Chinese Characters

（一）汉字的结构（3） Structures of Chinese characters (3)

上下、左右、包围是汉字的三种基本结构形式，以这三种结构为基础，可以派生出很多更复杂的形式。如：

Top-bottom, left-right and enclosed are the three basic types of character structure, on the bases of which, quite a number of more complicated types may be derived. For example:

上下结构的派生　Derivation of top-bottom structure:

上中下
Top-middle-bottom

1
2
3

客　堂

上下里含有左右
Top-bottom with left-right inside

1	
2	3

宿　花

1	2
3	

留　努

左右结构的派生　Derivation of left-right structure:

左中右
Left-middle-right

1	2	3

谢　难

左右里含有上下
Left-right with top-bottom inside

1	2
	3

语　请

1	3
2	

教　新

　　这些结构还可以派生出更复杂的结构，我们就不再一一举例了。要写好汉字，一定要注意汉字的结构。学写汉字时，看到一个新的汉字，首先要仔细观察，从总体上把握好这个汉字的结构，这样才能把汉字写得匀称、好看。

　　Many more complicated types of structures can be derived from these structures. Examples won't be given any more. To write Chinese characters well, one must pay attention to their structures. To write a Chinese character, first, one must watch the new character carefully so as to learn the general structure of the character. Then the character can be written symmetrically and beautifully.

（二）笔画（4）：派生笔画　　Strokes (4) : Derivative strokes

1. ㇋ :（乙）　横折折　héngzhézhé　horizontal-zag-zag
   例字：没　沿

2. 乛 :（乛）　横折弯钩（2）　héngzhéwāngōu　horizontal-zag-clockwise curve-J hook
   例字：都　院

3. 乙 :（乙）　横折弯钩（3）　héngzhéwāngōu　horizontal-zag-anticlockwise curve-J hook
   例字：吃　乙

4. ㇌ :（㇌）　横折折折钩　héngzhézhégōu　horizontal-zag-zag-zag-J hook
   例字：场　汤

5. ㇗ :（㇗）　竖折　shùzhé　vertical-zag
   例字：每　画

（三）笔顺（3）：先外后内再关门，先中间后两边

Stroke orders (3) : First outside, second inside and then door-closed; first middle and then two sides

规则五：先外后内再关门

Rule 5:　First outside, second inside and then door-closed

半包围结构的汉字一般要先写外面后写里面。如：

For characters of half-enclosed structue, usually outside first and inside second. For example:

左上包围：　　店→广　店　　　　　　右上包围：　　习→㇆　习

Left-top enclosed　　　　　　　　　　　　　Right-top enclosed

左上右包围：　　同→冂　同

Left-top-right enclosed

但是，有左下方包围的偏旁或左下右包围的部件字要先写里面再写外面。如：

Sometimes, a character should be written inside first and outside second when it is of left-bottom enclosed or of left-bottom-right enclosed. For example:

左下：　　　　这→辶 这　　　　左下右：　　画→凵 画

Left-bottom　　　　　　　　　　　Left-bottom-right

全包围结构的字要先写左上右的半包围框架，再写里面的部分，最后写关门的横。如：

As for the characters of fully enclosed structure, the left-top-right structure should be written first, then the inside structure and finally the last horizontal stroke. For example:

国：冂 囯 国　　　　　　四：冂 四 四

规则六：先中间后两边　　Rule 6: First middle and then two sides

如果竖和由竖组成的笔画在中间，两边各有相应的部分，而且竖画不跟其他的笔画相交或者竖画下面有阻挡的其他笔画，那么，应该先写中间的竖，再写两边的笔画。如：

If a vertical stroke or its derivation is in the middle with vertically symmetrical strokes on both sides, and the vertical stroke does not intersect with others, or any obstruct stroke is under the vertical stroke, then, the middle stroke should be written first and then strokes on both sides.

小：亅 小　　　　　　　　山：丨 山
水：亅 水　　　　　　　　当：丨 丷 当

但是，如果竖与其他笔画相交叉，那么，应该遵守其他相关规则。如：

However, if the vertical stroke intersects with others, then other concerned rules ought to be obeyed.

中：口 中　　　　　　　　土：一 十 土

（四）怎样避免写错汉字（４）：注意笔画关系

Avoiding writing mistakes (4) : Pay attention to the relations of strokes

每个汉字笔画与笔画之间的关系是固定的。广义的笔画间关系包括几个方面。其中一个就是我们前面所说的相离、相接、相交关系，不能随意改变，否则就是错别字。如：

Every Chinese character has its own fixed stroke relations. General stroke relations include several aspects. The one is the relations of separating, connecting and intersecting. It can't be changed at random, or it is a wrong character. For example:

刀 (dāo) — 力 (lì)　　工 (gōng) — 土 (tǔ)　　天 (tiān) — 夫 (fū)

另外，还要注意笔画之间的上下关系，这一点也千万不能搞错。如：

What's more, pay attention to the up-and-down relation of strokes. For example:

人（rén）——入（rù）

六 练习 Exercises

（一）认读声韵母并比较异同 Read and identify the following initials and finals

z — zh　　　c — ch　　　s — sh　　　r

ua — uo　　uai — uei　　uan — uang　　uen — ueng

（二）声调练习 Tones

zān — zán — zǎn — zàn　　　　zhē — zhé — zhě — zhè
cī — cí — cǐ — cì　　　　　　sōng — sóng — sǒng — sòng
rāng — ráng — rǎng — ràng　　chū — chú — chǔ — chù
shēn — shén — shěn — shèn　　wān — wán — wǎn — wàn

（三）认读音节并比较异同 Read and identify the syllables

sùshè — shūshì　　　cùnduàn — cáituán　　　chuāiduó — chuīdǎ
cáichǎn — chāi sàn　zhuózhuàng — cūzhuāng　cāngcuì — zhuāng shuǐ
zīshēn — zhíchēng　zhuāngzài — chuāngtái　shēncháng — shēngchǎn

（四）认读并连线 Read, learn and match

这　　　　diǎn　　　　　堂　　　　shì
是　　　　qù　　　　　　宿　　　　jiàn
回　　　　cí　　　　　　什　　　　jiào
词　　　　huí　　　　　 教　　　　shén
典　　　　zhè　　　　　 见　　　　táng
舍　　　　shè　　　　　 早　　　　zǎo
去　　　　shì　　　　　 室　　　　sù

(五) 认读词语或句子　　Read and learn the phrases or sentences

你好　　不太忙　　什么　　宿舍　　请进　　你的书　　谢谢　　不客气
汉语难吗？　　　今天星期几？　　　我有英语课。　　　你去哪儿？

(六) 写音节　　Write out the syllables

uo → ____　　　uai → ____　　　uen → ____　　　uang → ____

d + iou → ____　　　t + uei → ____　　　l + uen → ____

l + iou (ˊ) → ____　　　　　　　　j + iou (ˋ) → ____

d + uei (ˉ) → ____　　　　　　　　c + uei (ˇ) → ____

(七) 汉字练习　　Writing Chinese characters

1. 描写笔画　　Trace the following strokes

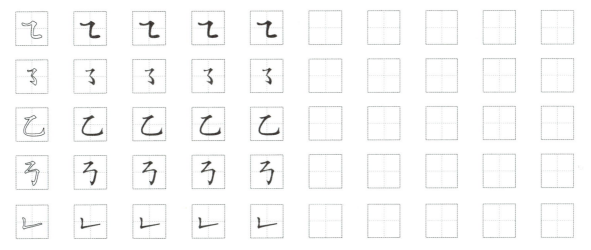

2. 描写汉字　　Trace the following characters

3．写出下列汉字的笔画数　Write out the amount of stokes of the following characters

　　词（　　）　这（　　）　么（　　）　回（　　）　哪（　　）

4．写出包括下列笔画的汉字（选做）Write out the Chinese characters including the following strokes (optional)

　　乚：_____　　　　了：_____

　　乙：_____　　　　㇠：_____

　　㇄：_____

5．写出下列汉字的笔顺　Write out the stroke orders of the following characters

　　的：_____　　　　回：_____

　　堂：_____　　　　再：_____

　　这：_____　　　　早：_____

6．写出五个上下结构的汉字　Write out five characters including top-bottom structures

　　□　□　□　□　□

7．临写本课笔画、汉字并比较与以前所学笔画间的异同　Copy the strokes and characters learnt in this lesson, and compare to those learnt before

文化小贴士　Proverb

Shào zhuàng bù nǔ lì,　lǎo dà tú shāng bēi.
少　壮　不　努力，　老　大　徒　伤　悲。

A young idler, an old beggar.

第五课
复习（一）

Lesson 5 — Review (I)

一 》 生 词 New Words

1.	国	n.	guó	country
2.	人	n.	rén	people, human being
3.	二	num.	èr	two
4.	零	num.	líng	zero
5.	一	num.	yī	one
6.	年	n.	nián	year
7.	十月	n.	shíyuè	October
8.	出生	v.	chūshēng	be born
9.	明天	n.	míngtiān	tomorrow
10.	生日	n.	shēngrì	birthday
11.	留学生	n.	liúxuéshēng	student studying abroad, international student
12.	学习	v.	xuéxí	learn, study

13.	老师	n.	lǎoshī	teacher
14.	现在	n.	xiànzài	now

专名 Proper Nouns

1.	英国	Yīngguó	Britain, the United Kingdom
2.	张	Zhāng	a surname

本课新字 New Characters

国　人　二　年　十　月　出　生
明　日　留　学　习　师　现　在

二 课文 Text

汉语不太难

Nǐ hǎo! Wǒ shì Yīngguórén. Wǒ èrlínglíngyī nián
你好！我是英国人。我二零零一年
shíyuè chūshēng, míngtiān shì wǒ de shēngrì.
十月出生，明天是我的生日。
Wǒ shì liúxuéshēng, wǒ hěn máng. Wǒ xuéxí
我是留学生，我很忙。我学习
Hànyǔ, Hànyǔ bú tài nán. Wǒ yǒu Hànyǔshū、Hànyǔ
汉语，汉语不太难。我有汉语书、汉语
cídiǎn. Wǒ de lǎoshī shì Zhāng lǎoshī, Zhāng lǎoshī hěn hǎo.
词典。我的老师是张老师，张老师很好。
Jīntiān xīngqīwǔ, wǒ yǒu Hànyǔkè. Xiànzài, wǒ qù jiàoshì. Zàijiàn!
今天星期五，我有汉语课。现在，我去教室。再见！

三 注释 Notes

"一"的变调　Modulations of "一"

"一"的本调是第一声。在单用、数数、读号码或词语末尾时用本调第一声。在其他情况下，"一"的声调会发生改变：

Basically, "一" is the first tone. When read alone, or in counting or in numbers, its basic tone is read. Under other circumstances, "一" may be modulated:

1．在第一、第二、第三声前面，读第四声。如：

It pronounced as the 4th tone followed by the 1st, the 2nd and the 3rd tones. For example:

| yìbān | yìxiē | yì tiān | yìshēng | yìlián | yìtóng |
| yì nián | yìzhí | yìqǐ | yì shǒu | yì zhǒng | yì kǒu |

2．在第四声前面，读第二声。如：

It pronounced as the 2nd tone followed by the 4th tone. For example:

| yígài | yílù | yízhì | yídìng | yídào | yígòng |
| yíhuàng | yímiàn |

3．在重叠的单音节动词中间，读轻声。如：

It pronounced as a neutral tone in the middle of reduplicated single-syllable verbs. For example:

tīng yi tīng　shuō yi shuō　dú yi dú　tán yi tán　xiě yi xiě　zǒu yi zǒu

四 练习 Exercises

（一）认读声韵母并比较异同．Read and identify the following initials and finals

b—p:　bóbo — pópo　　bàopò — pùbù
　　　bǎo le — pǎo le　bèifèn — pèibèi

d—t:　dìdi — tiāntiān　dàitì — dìtú
　　　diǎndī — diàntī　dútè — tóuděng

g—k:　gēge — kěkě　　gōngkè — kǎigē
　　　bù gǎi — bù kāi　kuānguǎng — kāngkǎi

j—q:　　jījí　　— qīnqiè　　　　qìnghè — jìnghè
　　　　jīqì　　— qǐjū　　　　　jǔzhòng — qǐzhòng

zh—ch:　zhīdao — chídào　　　　zhīchí — chéngzhèn
　　　　zhīzhū — chǎnchē

z—c:　　zǎocāo — cìzǐ　　　　　zōngzú — cāngcù
　　　　zǐdì — cìdì　　　　　　dà zǎo — dǎ cǎo

（二）声调练习　　Tones

bāfāng	bāxiān	bāguà	bājiāo	cóng'ér	cónglái
cóngqián	cóngróng	dǎngǎn	dǎnxiǎo	dǎdǎo	dǎ sǎn
dàihào	dàduì	nèihào	nèijiù	pānyuán	pānzhé
qūshǐ	qūjiě	qīdài	qīmò	jíxū	jíjiāng
jí diǎn	jípǐn	yíhàn	yíxùn	lèguān	lètiān
mièjué	miàolíng	shànjǔ	shànkuǎn		

（三）变调　　Modulations

1. mǎpǐ　　fǔdǎo　　kǎogǔ　　kǒuyǔ　　běibiān　　xǔduō
   qiǎntān　lǚxíng　　lǎodà　　jiǎngtái　　bǎncái　　gǎnxiè
   wǔ xià　　tiělù　　kěnqiè

2. búbì　　búdàn　　búgòu　　búpèi　　chī bu chī　　kàn bu kàn
   shuō bu shuō

3. yì tiān　yìshēng　yìtóng　yì nián　yìqǐ　yì kǒu
   yízhì　yídìng　dú yi dú　xiě yi xiě

（四）认一认，读一读　　Read and learn

一　二　三　四　五　六　七　八　九　十

你好　　　　　早上好　　　　你好吗　　　　很好
谢谢　　　　　不客气　　　　汉语难吗　　　不太忙
这是什么　　　汉语词典　　　今天星期几　　我有英语课
我去教室　　　再见

(五) 写音节 Write out the syllables

i → _____   ie → _____   iou → _____   in → _____   iong → _____

u → _____   ua → _____   uei → _____   uo → _____   uang → _____

ü → _____   üe → _____   uen → _____

jia (ˉ) → _____   gei (ˇ) → _____   dao (ˋ) → _____

tai (ˋ) → _____   tou (ˊ) → _____   ji (ˊ) → _____

j + u (ˉ) → _____   q + u (ˋ) → _____   qi (ˋ) → _____

n + u (ˇ) → _____   l + u (ˋ) → _____   xi (ˉ) → _____

j + iou (ˇ) → _____   d + uei (ˋ) → _____   t + uen (ˊ) → _____

(六) 汉字练习 Writing Chinese Characters

1. 描写汉字 Trace the following characters

2. 写出下列汉字的笔画数　Write out the amount of strokes of the following characters

英（　） 国（　） 出（　） 留（　） 书（　）

3. 写出包括下列笔画的汉字（选做）Write out some characters including the following strokes (optional)

一：_____　　　ノ：_____

丿：_____　　　㇆：_____

丶：_____　　　㇆：_____

㇏：_____　　　乚：_____

亅：_____　　　㇜：_____

㇉：_____　　　㇌：_____

4. 写出下列汉字的笔顺　Write out the stroke orders of the following characters

国：_____　　年：_____

月：_____　　日：_____

习：_____　　生：_____

5. 按部首给下列汉字归类　Sort the following characters on the radicals

你　好　这　什　词　宿　忙　语　哪
英　吗　法　进　客　谢　课　他　请

亻：_____　　女：_____　　忄：_____

艹：_____　　辶：_____　　口：_____

讠：_____　　宀：_____　　氵：_____

文化小贴士　Proverb

Dú zài yìxiāng wéi yì kè, měi féng jiājié bèi sī qīn.
独在异乡为异客，每逢佳节倍思亲。

Alone, a lonely stranger in a strange land,
I pine for my kinfolks on holidays very much.

汉字笔画表
Strokes of Chinese Characters

笔画 Strokes	名称 Names of Strokes		运笔方向 Stroke Directions	例字 Example Characters		
一	横 héng		→	一	五	白
丨	竖 shù		↓	白	不	口
丿	撇 piě		↙	八	大	你
㇏	捺 nà		↘	八	大	太
丶	点 diǎn		↘	不	爸	弟
㇀	提 tí		↗	法	习	我
㇕	折 zhé	横折 héngzhé	㇕	五	口	的
㇄		竖折 shùzhé	㇄	出	区	医
㇆	钩 gōu	横钩 hénggōu	㇆	客	买	皮
亅		竖钩 shùgōu	亅	小	丁	寸
㇁		弯钩 wāngōu	㇁	家	狗	象
㇂		斜钩 xiégōu	㇂	我	钱	成
㇃		平钩 pínggōu	㇃	心	必	
㇇	撇点 piědiǎn		㇇	好	她	
㇉	横折钩 héngzhégōu		㇉	也	她	
㇌	竖弯钩 shùwāngōu		㇌	儿	他	
㇋	竖折折钩 shùzhézhégōu		㇋	马	弟	
㇅	横撇 héngpiě		㇅	又	汉	
㇋	横折折撇 héngzhézhépiě		㇋	进	这	
㇊	横折提 héngzhétí		㇊	语	请	
㇈	横折弯钩 héngzhéwāngōu	(1)	㇈	九	几	
乙		(2)	乙	吃	乙	
㇋		(3)	㇋	那	陪	
㇜	撇折 piězhé		㇜	法	么	
㇍	横折折 héngzhézhé		㇍	没	沿	
㇎	横折折折钩 héngzhézhézhégōu		㇎	场	汤	

汉字笔顺规则表

Rules of Chinese Character Stroke Orders

例 字 Example Characters	笔 顺 Stroke Orders	规 则 Rules
二	一 二	先上后下
八	丿 八	先左后右
十	一 十	先横后竖
人	丿 人	先撇后捺
应	丶 亠 广 广 应 应	先外后内
习	乛 冫 习	
问	丶 亻 门 门 问 问	
国	丨 冂 冂 冃 囝 国 国 国	先外后内再封口
小	亅 小 小	先中间后两边

第六课
我们都喜欢汉语

Lesson 6
We all like Chinese

这一课你将学到

语法项目 Grammar

1. 动词谓语句
   我学习汉语。

2. "是"字句
   我是／不是老师。

3. 疑问句（1）：吗
   您是张老师吗？

4. 疑问句（2）：什么
   你叫什么名字？

重点词语 Key Words

1. 副词"也"　　（他是学生，）我也是学生。

2. 副词"不"　　我不学习汉语。

3. 副词"都"　　我们都学习汉语。

功能项目 Activities

打招呼、询问

一 ▶ 生词 New Words

1.	您	*pron.*	nín	you
2.	学生	*n.*	xuésheng	student, pupil
3.	叫	*v.*	jiào	be called
4.	名字	*n.*	míngzi	name
5.	姓	*n./v.*	xìng	surname, family name; name
6.	高兴	*adj.*	gāoxìng	glad, happy
7.	认识	*v.*	rènshi	know, be familiar with
8.	和	*conj.*	hé	and
9.	那	*pron.*	nà	that
10.	笔	*n.*	bǐ	pen, pencil, writing brush
11.	本子	*n.*	běnzi	book, notebook
12.	书包	*n.*	shūbāo	schoolbag
13.	他	*pron.*	tā	he, him
14.	朋友	*n.*	péngyou	friend
15.	都	*adv.*	dōu	all
16.	喜欢	*v.*	xǐhuan	like, love, be fond of

专名 Proper Nouns

1.	丁荣	Dīng Róng	name of a person
2.	王明	Wáng Míng	name of a person
3.	波伟	Bōwěi	name of a person

本课新字 New Characters

学　叫　姓　和　那　笔　本
子　包　他　朋　都　喜　欢

二 课文 Texts

（一）您是张老师吗

Dīng Róng: Nín hǎo!
丁荣：您好！

Wáng Míng: Nǐ hǎo!
王明：你好！

Dīng Róng: Nín shì Zhāng lǎoshī ma?
丁荣：您是张老师吗？

Wáng Míng: Bù, wǒ bú shì lǎoshī, wǒ yě shì xuésheng. Tā shì Zhāng lǎoshī.
王明：不，我不是老师，我也是学生。他是张老师。

Dīng Róng: Xièxie nín!
丁荣：谢谢您！

Wáng Míng: Bú xiè.
王明：不谢。

Dīng Róng: Zhāng lǎoshī, nín hǎo!
丁荣：张老师，您好！

Zhāng lǎoshī: Nǐ hǎo! Nǐ jiào shénme míngzi?
张老师：你好！你叫什么名字？

Dīng Róng: Wǒ xìng Dīng, jiào Dīng Róng.
丁荣：我姓丁，叫丁荣。

Hěn gāoxìng rènshi nín.
很高兴认识您。

Zhāng lǎoshī: Rènshi nǐ wǒ yě hěn gāoxìng.
张老师：认识你我也很高兴。

（二）我们都喜欢汉语

Wǒ shì xuésheng. Wǒ xìng Dīng, jiào Dīng Róng. Wǒ xuéxí Hànyǔ. Zhè shì
我是学生。我姓丁，叫丁荣。我学习汉语。这是
wǒ de Hànyǔshū hé Hànyǔ cídiǎn, nà shì wǒ de bǐ、 běnzi hé shūbāo.
我的汉语书和汉语词典，那是我的笔、本子和书包。
Tā jiào Bōwěi, shì wǒ de péngyou. Tā yě shì xuésheng, yě xuéxí Hànyǔ.
他叫波伟，是我的朋友。他也是学生，也学习汉语。
Wǒmen dōu xuéxí Hànyǔ, wǒmen dōu xǐhuan Hànyǔ.
我们都学习汉语，我们都喜欢汉语。

三 注释 Notes

（一）姓和名字　Surname and given name

中国人的姓名一般是姓在前面，名字在后面。如"王小英"，其中"王"是姓，"小英"是名。右表中有中国人常用的姓。

In names of Chinese, the surname is placed in front of the given name. Such as "王小英", among which "王" is surname, while "小英" is the given name. The frequently used surnames in China are in the right-hand list.

姓	拼音
王	Wáng
张	Zhāng
李	Lǐ
刘	Liú
赵	Zhào
马	Mǎ
金	Jīn

（二）"谢谢你""不谢"　"Thank you" and "Not at all"

表示感谢一般用"谢谢""谢谢你"。回答的时候可以说"不谢""不用谢""不客气"。
"谢谢" and "谢谢你" usually express one's thanks. The answers are "不谢""不用谢" and "不客气".

四 》 汉字知识 About Chinese Characters

（一）怎样写好汉字（1）：横平竖直
Write characters beautifully (1): Level horizontal and upright vertical

横和竖是汉字的基本笔画。书写时，横，要写得平，右边可以稍稍比左边高一点儿。如："一"。但一定不能写得左高右低，如"一"。竖，一般是垂直的。

Horizontal and vertical are the basic strokes of Chinese characters. In writing, the horizontal should be level, the right end is a slightly higher than that of left, for example: "一", but not vise verse, for example: "一". Vertical is usually upright.

横和竖是汉字最重要的笔画，起支撑的作用，就像人的骨架、房子的梁柱。横和竖如果写得不平不直，字就会歪斜，给人不平衡、要倒下来的感觉。如"十"。所以，写好汉字要记住的第一条规则是——横平竖直。

Horizontal and vertical are also the most important strokes in Chinese. They are the supporters in characters as the bones of a body and the beams in a house. If the horizontal is not smooth, or the vertical is not upright, the character is lean, which gives an impression that the character is not balanced and will fall down, for example: "十". Therefore smooth horizontal and upright vertical is the first rule to keep in mind in writing a character.

（二）偏旁：女、讠 Radicals: "女" and "讠"

构成合体字的部分叫作偏旁。如"好"中的"女"和"子"，"妈"中的"女"和"马"都是偏旁。偏旁分形旁和声旁两种。如"妈"中的"女"是形旁，表示意义，"马"是声旁，与读音有关。

Part of a multi-component character is called the radical. For example, "女" and "子" in "好", "女" and "马" in "妈" are radicals. Radicals can be divided into semantic component and phonetic component. For example, the radical "女" in the character "妈" is a semantic component, indicating the meaning; and the radical "马" is a semantic component, indicating its pronunciation.

做偏旁的，有的是独体字，如"马"；有的是从独体字演变来的，如"法"中的"氵"。

Some radicals are single-component characters, such as "马"; some are derived from single-component, such as "氵" in "法".

从本课开始，我们将陆续介绍汉字的常用偏旁，着重介绍表示意义的形旁，以帮助大家更好地掌握汉字。

From this lesson, we will study the frequently used radicals of characters, focusing on the semantic components representing some certain meanings so as to learn Chinese well.

1. 女
女字旁
nǚzìpáng

用在字的左边或下边，位于左边时，写作"女"；位于下边时，写作"女"。女字旁的字一般与妇女有关。如："好、要"。
Radical "女" is placed on the left or at the bottom. It is written as "女" on the left, and "女" at the bottom. Usually characters with this radical are related to women. For example: "好，要".

2. 讠
言字旁
yánzìpáng

用在字的左边或中间。言字旁的字都与语言有关。如："谢、语、辩(biàn)"。
Radical "讠" is placed on the left or in the middle, which is interrelated with the language. For example: "谢" "语" and "辩 (biàn)".

五 语 法 Grammar

（一）动词谓语句 Sentences with verbal predicates

汉语的基本语序是"主语（S）+ 谓语（V）+ 宾语（O）"，这一点要特别注意。
The basic order of a Chinese sentence is "subject + predicate + object". It ought to be kept in mind.

| 主语 | + | 谓语 | + | 宾语 |
subject		predicate		object
我		叫		丁荣。
我		学习		汉语。

（二）"是"字句　是-sentence

"是"字句一般表示判断，常见结构是"A＋是＋B"，否定形式是"A＋不是＋B"。

Usually, the 是- sentence indicates judgement. The usual structure is "A is B". The negative one is "A is not B".

A	是	B	→	A	不是	B
A	is	B.		A	is not	B
她	是	老师。	→	她	不是	老师。
我	是	学生。	→	我	不是	学生。

（三）疑问句（1）：用"吗"的疑问句
Interrogative sentences (1) : Questions with "吗"

"吗"加在陈述句的末尾，用来表示疑问。如：
Questions in which "吗" is added to the end of a declarative sentence. For example:

(1) 她是老师。→ 她是老师吗?

(2) 我是学生。→ 你是学生吗?

（四）疑问句（2）：用"什么"提问
Interrogative sentences (2) : Questions with "什么"

"什么"是一个疑问代词，可以用来询问。用"什么"提问的时候，不改变句子原来的语序。如：

"什么" is an interrogative pronoun. It is used to inquire. When a question is asked by "什么", the original sentence order is not changed. For example：

(1) A：你学习什么?　　B：我学习汉语。

(2) A：你叫什么名字?　　B：我叫王小英。

六 重点词语 Key Words

（一）副词"也"　　Adverb "也"

"也"是副词，表示两事相同。一般来说，前后两句话的谓语相同、主语不同时，后一句话的主语后面要用"也"。如：

"也" is an adverb, which means that two things are the same. Generally, if the predicative verbs of two clauses are the same, while their subjects are not the same, then "也" should be used after the subject of the later clause. For example：

(1) 你学习汉语，我也学习汉语。

(2) 你是学生，我也是学生。

（二）副词"不"　　Adverb "不"

"不"是一个副词，用在动词、形容词或个别副词前，表示否定。

"不" is an adverb. It can be used in front of the verbs, adjectives, or a few adverbs, expressing negative meaning.

主语	+	不	+	谓语	+	……
subject	+	不	+	predicate	+	…
我		不		学习		汉语。
她		不		去。		

（三）副词"都"　　Adverb "都"

"都"是一个副词，用在动词或形容词前边，表示总括。

"都" is an adverb. It can be used in front of an adjective or a verb to sum up the preceding elements.

主语	+	都	+	谓语	+	……
subject	+	都	+	predicate	+	…
我们		都		是		学生。
我们		都		学习		汉语。

七 >> 练 习 Exercises

（一）认读汉字并写出拼音   Read and learn the following characters and give *pinyin* to each of them

姓（　）　　叫（　）　　和（　）　　那（　）　　笔（　）

本（　）　　包（　）　　都（　）　　喜（　）　　欢（　）

（二）朗读下面的短语   Read the following phrases

学习汉语	学习英语	喜欢汉语	喜欢中国	喜欢他
是老师	是学生	什么名字	什么书	什么笔
姓丁	姓张	不是	不喜欢	不高兴

（三）替换练习   Substitution

1. A：你学习什么？
   B：我学习汉语。

   英语
   法语
   数学（shùxué mathematics）
   物理（wùlǐ physics）
   化学（huàxué chemistry）

2. A：你叫什么名字？
   B：我叫丁荣。

   王英（Wáng Yīng）
   张强（Zhāng Qiáng）
   李芳（Lǐ Fāng）

3. 这是书。

   本子
   笔
   橡皮（xiàngpí rubber）

(四)把"是"字句改成否定形式　Change the following sentences into negative sentences

1．我是学生。　_____

2．他是老师。　_____

3．他是我同学。　_____

4．这是书。　_____

5．那是词典。　_____

(五)把下列句子改成用"吗"的疑问句　Change the following sentences into questions with "吗"

1．你好。　_____

2．她是王小英。　_____

3．我是学生。　_____

4．我学习汉语。　_____

5．他喜欢英语。　_____

(六)用"什么"提问　Change the following sentences into questions with "什么"

1．他学习汉语。　_____

2．他喜欢英语。　_____

3．我叫丁荣。　_____

4．我姓王。　_____

5．这是书。　_____

(七)选词填空　Choose and fill in the blanks

也　不　是　和　叫　都

你好！我_____丁荣。我_____学生，我学习汉语。他叫波伟，他_____是学生。他_____学习英语，他_____学习汉语。我_____他学习_____很努力。

（八）连词成句 Make sentences with the given words

1. 叫 我 王英 → _____。

2. 你 认识 很高兴 → _____。

3. 我 老师 是 不 → _____。

4. 吗 你 也 学习 汉语 → _____。

5. 名字 你 叫 什么 → _____。

（九）用下列偏旁写出至少三个汉字 Write out at least three characters with the following radicals

女：_____   讠：_____

（十）描写汉字 Trace the following characters

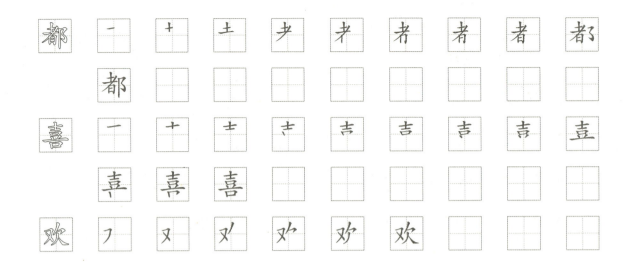

文化小贴士 Proverb

Jìngyèsī
静夜思

(Táng) Lǐ Bái
(唐) 李白

Chuáng qián míngyuè guāng, yí shì dìshàng shuāng.
床前明月光，疑是地上霜。
Jǔ tóu wàng míngyuè, dī tóu sī gùxiāng.
举头望明月，低头思故乡。

A Tranquil Night

(Tang Dynasty) Li Bai

In front of my bed, I see a silver light,

I wonder if it's frost aground.

Looking up, I find the moon bright,

bowing, in homesickness I'm drowned.

第七课
你们班有多少个学生

Lesson 7

How many students are there in your class

这一课你将学到

语法项目 Grammar

1. "有"字句

   我们班有十七个学生。

2. 称数法（1）：百以内的数字

   十七　十六

3. 数量短语

   三位老师　十七个学生

4. 疑问句（3）：特指问句"多少""几"和"谁"

   你们班有多少个学生？

   你们有几位老师？

   谁是你们的语法老师？

5. 状语（1）：副词做状语

   他们也都学习汉语。

功能项目 Activity

询问数量（1）：询问百以内的数字

一 生词 New Words

1.	你们	pron.	nǐmen	you
2.	班	n.	bān	class
3.	多少	pron.	duōshao	how much, how many
4.	个	m.	gè	a general measure word for nouns
5.	对	adj.	duì	right, correct
6.	我们	pron.	wǒmen	we, us
7.	位	m.	wèi	used before people
8.	谁	pron.	shéi	who, whom
9.	语法	n.	yǔfǎ	grammar
10.	今年	n.	jīnnián	this year
11.	岁	m.	suì	year (of age), year
12.	国家	n.	guójiā	country, nation, state
13.	他们	pron.	tāmen	they, them
14.	两	num.	liǎng	two
15.	一起	adv.	yìqǐ	together, in company, altogether
16.	玩儿	v.	wánr	play, play with, toy with
17.	教	v.	jiāo	teach, instruct, tutor
18.	听力	n.	tīnglì	listening
19.	口语	n.	kǒuyǔ	spoken language

专名 Proper Nouns

1.	北京大学	Běijīng Dàxué	Peking University
2.	王	Wáng	a surname
3.	田	Tián	a surname

本课新字 New Characters

| 班 | 多 | 少 | 个 | 对 | 位 | 谁 |
| 岁 | 家 | 两 | 起 | 玩 | 听 | 力 |

二 课 文 Texts

（一）你们班有多少个学生

A：Nǐ shì xuésheng ma?
你是学生吗？

B：Duì, wǒ shì Běijīng Dàxué de liúxuéshēng.
对，我是北京大学的留学生。

A：Nǐ shì jǐ bān de xuésheng?
你是几班的学生？

B：Wǒ shì èr bān de xuésheng.
我是二班的学生。

A：Nǐmen bān yǒu duōshao ge xuésheng?
你们班有多少个学生？

B：Wǒmen bān yǒu shíqī ge xuésheng.
我们班有十七个学生。

A：Nǐmen yǒu jǐ wèi lǎoshī?
你们有几位老师？

Wǒmen yǒu sān wèi lǎoshī.
B：我们 有 三 位 老师。

Shéi shì nǐmen de yǔfǎ lǎoshī?
A：谁 是 你们 的 语法 老师？

Zhāng lǎoshī shì wǒmen de yǔfǎ lǎoshī.
B：张 老师 是 我们 的 语法 老师。

（二）我们班有十六个国家的学生

Wǒ jīnnián shíbā suì, shì Běijīng Dàxué de liúxuéshēng, wǒ xuéxí Hànyǔ.
我 今年 十八 岁，是 北京 大学 的 留学生，我 学习 汉语。
Wǒmen bān yǒu shíliù ge guójiā de xuésheng, tāmen yě dōu xuéxí Hànyǔ. Wǒ yǒu
我们 班 有 十六 个 国家 的 学生，他们 也 都 学习 汉语。我 有
liǎng ge hǎo péngyou, wǒmen yìqǐ xuéxí, yìqǐ wánr, rènshi tāmen wǒ hěn
两 个 好 朋友，我们 一起 学习，一起 玩儿，认识 他们 我 很
gāoxìng. Wǒmen yǒu sān wèi lǎoshī, Zhāng lǎoshī jiāo yǔfǎ, Wáng lǎoshī jiāo tīng
高兴。我们 有 三 位 老师，张 老师 教 语法，王 老师 教 听
lì, Tián lǎoshī jiāo kǒuyǔ. Wǒ hěn xǐhuan tāmen.
力，田 老师 教 口语。我 很 喜欢 他们。

三 注释 Note

对，我是北京大学的留学生。 Yes, I am a foreign student of Peking University.

形容词"对"用来表示赞成对方的说法或回答别人的问题。回答时可以直接回答"对"，也可以把前面的内容重复一遍。如：

The adjective "对" (yes, right) is an approval to a statement or a definite answer. One may answer "对" directly, or repeat the previous statement. For example:

(1) A：张老师是一位很好的老师。
　　B：对。

(2) A：你是北京大学的学生吗？
　　B：对，我是北京大学的学生。

四 汉字知识 About Chinese Characters

（一）怎样写好汉字（2）：横平竖直
Write characters beautifully (2) : Level horizontal and upright vertical

如果把一个汉字比作一座房子，那么"横"就是"梁"，"竖"就是"柱"。"横"和"竖"写得好不好，对一个字写得正不正，稳不稳，有很重要的关系。

If a Chinese character is compared to a house, a horizontal stroke is the beam and the vertical stroke is the pillar. Whether the horizontal or the vertical strokes are written well is very important to the uprightness and balance of a Chinese character.

所谓"横平"不是绝对地水平，而是略呈左低右高的斜势。如："一"。如果将"横"写得绝对水平，字就显得呆板。如："一"。

Level horizontal doesn't mean it is absolutely level, but a slightly lean, the right end is slightly higher than the left one, such as "一". If it is written absolutely horizontal, the character would look stiff, such as "一".

所谓"竖直"有两种情况，如果只是单一的"竖"则要求正、直，一般不能左右偏侧倾斜，如："中"不能写成"中"。如果一个字中有对称的两竖，是短竖的，一般呈上开下合之势，如："业、曲"，不能写成" 曲、业"；是长竖的，可以基本平行，但仍略呈上开下合之势。如："直"。

Upright vertical includes two types. If it is a single vertical, it must be upright, such as "中", which cannot be written as "中". If there are two balanced short vertical strokes, usually they are V-shape lean, such as "业, 曲", which cannot be written as "曲, 业". If they are two long verticals, they are generally parallel, but still a little V-shape lean, such as "直".

（二）偏旁：亻、宀　　Radicals: "亻" and "宀"

1. **亻** 单人旁 dānrénpáng

   用在字的左边，单人旁的字一般与人有关。如："你、他"。
   It is placed on the left of a character, which is about the human. For example: "你, 他".

2. **宀** 宝盖 bǎogài

   用在字的上面，带宝盖头的字都与房屋、覆盖有关。如："宿、家"。
   It is placed on the top of a character, which means a house or a cover. For example: "宿, 家".

五 语法 Grammar

（一）"有"字句　有-sentence

"有"字句一般表示拥有某人或某物，常见的结构是"A + 有 + B"，否定形式是"A + 没有 + B"。A 可以是代词，可以是指人的名词，也可以是地点名词或时间名词。

有-sentence means to own somebody or something. The common pattern is "A + 有 + B" (A has B), and the negative form is "A + 没有 + B" (A doesn't have B). A may be a pronoun, a noun of personal reference, nouns of time and locality.

A 有 B	→	A 没有 B
A has B		A doesn't have B
我有姐姐。	→	我没有姐姐。
弟弟有一本汉语书。	→	弟弟没有汉语书。
这个月有三十一天。	→	这个月没有三十一天。
图书馆有法语书。	→	图书馆没有法语书。

（二）称数法（1）：百以内的数字
Reading of numbers (1) : Numbers less than one hundred

汉语百以内的数字表达如下：
Numbers less than one hundred can be expressed as the following:

一　　二　　三　　四　　五　　六　　七　　八　　九　　十

十一　十二　十三　十四　十五　十六　十七　十八　十九　二十

二十一　二十二　二十三　二十四　二十五　二十六　二十七　二十八　二十九　三十

三十一 …………………………………………………………………… 四十

四十一 …………………………………………………………………… 九十九

（三）数量词组　Numeral-measure word phrases

量词是汉语中特有的一种词，经常和数词、名词组合构成数量词组，表示事物的数量。
Measure words are a kind of special words in Chinese. They often form phrases with numerals or nouns, meaning the amount of something.

数词	+	量词	+	名词
number	+	measure word	+	noun
三		个		国家
五		位		老师
六		本		书

（四）疑问句（3）：特指问句"多少""几"和"谁"
Interrogative sentences (3): Questions using interrogative pronouns: "多少" "几" and "谁"

"多少"和"几"都可以用来询问数量。"几"一般用于询问十以内的数量，"多少"一般用于询问十以上的数量。"几"后面一般要加量词，"多少"后面的量词可以省略。如：
Both "多少" and "几" can be used to ask the amount. Usually "几" is used to ask the amount less than ten, while "多少" asks the amount more than ten. There must be a measure word between "几" and a noun, while "多少" can be directly linked to a noun. For example:

(1) A：你有几个姐姐？

　　B：我有三个姐姐。

(2) A：你们班有多少（个）同学？

　　B：我们班有 17 个同学。

"谁"用来询问人物。如：
"谁" is used as an inquiry of a person. For example:

(1) A：谁是你们的语法老师？

　　B：张老师是我们的语法老师。

(2) A：那个人是谁？

　　B：他是波伟的哥哥。

（五）状语（1）：副词做状语
Adverbial adjuncts (1): Adverbs are used as adverbial adjuncts

状语在句子中主要修饰动词、形容词，表示动作进行的时间、处所、方式、范围以及性质、状态等。状语多由副词、形容词、介词短语和某些表示时间、地点的名词充当。本课我们学习的是副词做状语。副词做状语时，要放在谓语的前面。如：
The adverbial adjunct mainly modifies the verb or adjective in a sentence, expressing the time, location, manner, scope, nature and state of the action. Usually, an adverbial adjunct is acted by an adverb, an adjective, a prepositional phrase, or a noun of time or locality. This lesson focuses on the adverbs acting as adverbial adjuncts. When an adverb is acted as adverbial, the adverb must be put before the predicate. For example:

(1) 她<u>不</u>是学生。

(2) 爸爸<u>很</u>忙。

(3) 他<u>也</u>是学生。

(4) 他们<u>都</u>学习汉语。

这里，副词"不"用来表示否定，"很"表示程度，"也"和"都"表示范围。表示范围的"也"和"都"在句中做状语时可以同时出现，这时"也"一定要放在"都"的前面。如：

The adverb "不" expresses the negation, "很" expresses the degree. "也" and "都" express the scope, which may be acted as adverbial adjuncts at the same time in a sentence. In that case, "也" must be put before "都". For example:

(1) 我很忙，我的爸爸妈妈<u>也都</u>很忙。

(2) 我学习汉语，我的朋友<u>也都</u>学习汉语。

六 练习 Exercises

（一）朗读下面的短语　Read the following phrases

几位老师	几位朋友	多少（个）学生	多少个班
四位老师	八位朋友	七十八个学生	五十六个班
三个本子	六个书包	今年十岁	今年二十五岁
语法老师	听力老师	口语课	英语课
一起学习	一起去学校	一起回宿舍	一起来中国

（二）替换练习　Substitution

1. A：你有<u>姐姐</u>（jiějie, sister）吗？

   B：我有一<u>个</u> <u>姐姐</u>。

汉语书	本 (běn)
中国朋友	个
书包	个
笔	支 (zhī)

2. A：<u>你</u>有几个<u>书包</u>？
   B：我有<u>三</u>个<u>书包</u>。

你	哥哥	我	一个
你	朋友	我	四个
你们学校	食堂	我们学校	五个
她	本子	她	八个

3. A：<u>你们班</u>有多少个<u>学生</u>？
   B：我们班有<u>二十</u>个<u>学生</u>。

姐姐	中国朋友	姐姐	十五
你	本子	我	二十四
你们学校	班	我们学校	三十
你们学校	汉语老师	我们学校	四十五

4. A：谁是你们的口语老师？
   B：<u>王老师</u>是我们的口语老师。

张老师
田老师
丁老师
李 (Lǐ) 老师

（三）把"有"字句改成否定形式　Change the 有-sentences into its negative form

1. 我有一个姐姐。　_____。
2. 我们学校有留学生。　_____。
3. 他有汉语书。　_____。
4. 丁荣有中国朋友。　_____。
5. 他的妈妈有工作。　_____。

（四）用"多少""几"或"谁"就画线部分提问　According to the words underlined, ask questions with "多少""几" or "谁"

1. 这个学校有<u>五</u>个食堂。
2. <u>张老师</u>是我们的汉语老师。
3. 我们班有<u>三</u>位老师。

4. 我和波伟去教室。

5. 他们学校有二十个班。

6. 三班有八个男同学，六个女同学。

7. 丁荣是我的好朋友。

8. 我们班有十一个美国人。

（五）选词填空　Choose and fill in the blanks

一起　　谁　　玩儿　　岁　　国家　　教

1. ＿＿＿＿＿＿ 是你们的听力老师？

2. 今天，我和丁荣 ＿＿＿＿＿＿ 回宿舍。

3. 田老师 ＿＿＿＿＿＿ 什么？

4. 我们班有十一个 ＿＿＿＿＿＿ 的学生。

5. 今年我十九 ＿＿＿＿＿＿，弟弟十五 ＿＿＿＿＿＿。

6. 我喜欢和中国朋友一起 ＿＿＿＿＿＿。

（六）连词成句　Make sentences with the given words

1. 我　两个　有　中国朋友

　　＿＿＿＿＿＿＿＿＿＿＿＿＿＿＿＿

2. 多少　个　你们　留学生　有　班

　　＿＿＿＿＿＿＿＿＿＿＿＿＿＿＿＿

3. 几个　同学　女　你们班　有

　　＿＿＿＿＿＿＿＿＿＿＿＿＿＿＿＿

4. 都　汉语　他们　学习　也

　　＿＿＿＿＿＿＿＿＿＿＿＿＿＿＿＿

5. 我　很　认识　他们　高兴

　　＿＿＿＿＿＿＿＿＿＿＿＿＿＿＿＿

(七) 改错句　Correct the following sentences

1．你叫谁？

2．波伟有中国朋友三个。

3．你是什么名字？

4．我们去教室一起。

5．我很忙，我的朋友都也很忙。

6．我们班有二十学生。

(八) 用下列偏旁写出至少三个汉字　Write out at least three characters with the following radicals

亻：_____　　宀：_____

(九) 描写汉字　Trace the following characters

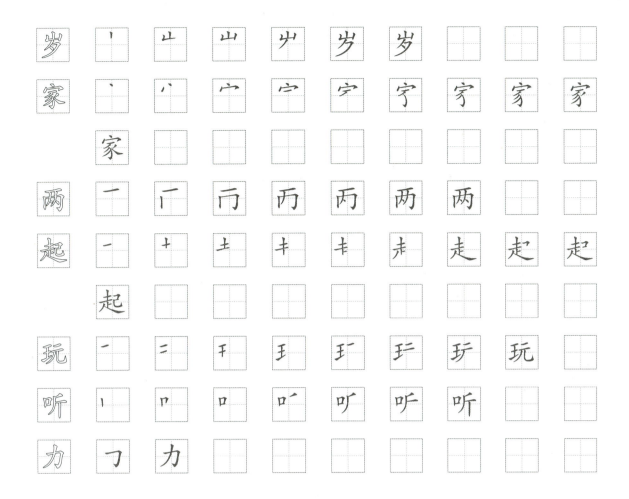

文化小贴士 Proverb

Wēn gù ér zhī xīn.
温故而知新。

Learn more by reviewing.

第八课
请问，留学生食堂在哪儿

Lesson 8

Excuse me, where is the dining hall for international students

这一课你将学到

语法项目　Grammar

1. 疑问句（4）：特指问句"哪儿""哪"
   留学生食堂在哪儿？
   你是哪国人？

2. 定语和助词"的"
   我是二班的学生。

3. 形容词谓语句
   她的汉语很好。

重点词语　Key Words

语气词"吧"
我们一起去吧。

功能项目　Activity

询问地点

一 》生词 New Words

1.	请问	v.	qǐngwèn	excuse me
2.	在	v./prep.	zài	be; in, on, at
3.	图书馆	n.	túshūguǎn	library
4.	后边	n.	hòubian	at the back, in the rear
5.	远	adj.	yuǎn	far away, distant
6.	吧	particle	ba	used at the end of a sentence, implying soliciting sb.'s advice, suggestion, request or mild command
7.	哪	pron.	nǎ	which
8.	看	v.	kàn	see, look at, watch
9.	黄色	n.	huángsè	yellow
	黄	adj.	huáng	yellow
	色	n.	sè	color
10.	楼	n.	lóu	building
11.	那儿	pron.	nàr	there
12.	不用	adv.	búyòng	need not
13.	新	adj.	xīn	new
14.	中午	n.	zhōngwǔ	noon, midday
15.	下午	n.	xiàwǔ	afternoon
16.	大	adj.	dà	big, large
17.	中文	n.	Zhōngwén	Chinese language
18.	英文	n.	Yīngwén	English
19.	晚上	n.	wǎnshang	evening, night

专名 Proper Nouns

1.	韩国	Hánguó	the Republic of Korea
2.	李明爱	Lǐ Míng'ài	name of a person
3.	美国	Měiguó	the United States of America
4.	安达	Āndá	name of a person

本课新字 New Characters

问　后　边　远　吧　看
黄　色　楼　用　文　晚

二 课文 Texts

（一）请问，留学生食堂在哪儿

Āndá: Qǐngwèn, liúxuéshēng shítáng zài nǎr?
安达：请问，留学生食堂在哪儿？

Lǐ Míng'ài: Zài túshūguǎn de hòubian.
李明爱：在图书馆的后边。

Āndá: Túshūguǎn zài nǎr? Yuǎn ma?
安达：图书馆在哪儿？远吗？

Lǐ Míng'ài: Bù yuǎn, wǒ qù túshūguǎn, wǒmen yìqǐ qù ba.
李明爱：不远，我去图书馆，我们一起去吧。

Āndá: Xièxie nǐ. Nǐ yě shì zhège xuéxiào de xuésheng ma?
安达：谢谢你。你也是这个学校的学生吗？

Lǐ Míng'ài: Duì, wǒ shì Hánguórén, jiào Lǐ Míng'ài. Nǐ shì nǎ guó rén?
李明爱：对，我是韩国人，叫李明爱。你是哪国人？

安达： 我是美国人，叫安达。

李明爱： 你是哪个班的学生？

安达： 我是二班的学生。

李明爱： 哪位老师教你们语法？

安达： 张老师教我们语法。他是一位很好的老师。

李明爱： 你看，这个黄色的大楼是图书馆，留学生食堂在那儿。

安达： 谢谢你。

李明爱： 不用谢。

（二）我有一个新朋友

我有一个新朋友，她叫李明爱，是韩国人。她也是我们学校的留学生，她的汉语很好。中午我和她一起去留学生食堂，下午我们一起去图书馆。

Wǒmen xuéxiào de túshūguǎn hěn dà, shū yě hěn duō, yǒu Zhōngwénshū, yě yǒu
我们 学校 的 图书馆 很 大，书 也 很 多，有 中文书，也 有
Yīngwénshū. Wǎnshang wǒmen yìqǐ huí sùshè. Jīntiān wǒ hěn gāoxìng.
英文书。晚上 我们 一起 回 宿舍。今天 我 很 高兴。

三 注释 Notes

请问，留学生食堂在哪儿？

Excuse me, where is the dining hall for international students?

"请问"是询问时的客气用语。

The word "请问" is a polite expression of an inquiry. For example:

(1) 请问，教室在哪儿？

(2) 请问，这是留学生宿舍吗？

四 汉字知识 About Chinese Characters

（一）怎样写好汉字（3）：疏密匀称

Write characters beautifully (3): Well-balanced structure

有的汉字笔画很少，如"乙"；有的汉字笔画很多，如"繁"。笔画少的汉字要写得宽舒、协调，如"一、十、大、千"。笔画多的汉字要写得紧密匀称，如"鲜、锻、镜、靠"。不能有的部分过紧，有的部分过松，如"繁"。尤其是有许多笔画连续平行排列时，要求每一笔之间的距离保持均匀，不能忽大忽小，忽松忽紧，如"直"。

Some characters have few strokes, such as "乙"; and some too many strokes, such as "繁". Characters with few strokes may be written loosely and coordinately, such as "一，十，大，千"; while those with many strokes may be written compactly, such as "鲜，锻，镜，靠". It is not good if some components of a character are written too compact while some too loose, such as "繁". Particularly for those characters with many parallel strokes written one after another, the space between two strokes should to be well-proportioned. It is not good if sometimes the space is big and loose, and sometimes small and compact, such as "直".

（二）偏旁：口、日　Radicals: "口" and "日"

1. 口
   口字旁
   kǒuzìpáng

   用在字的上边、下边、左边、右边或里边都可以，常常用于左边。口字旁的字都与口及口相关的器官、像口的东西有关。如："号、古、吗、和、可"。
   It can be placed at the top, bottom, left, right or inside of a character, but usually on the left. Characters with the radical "口" has the meaning of a mouth or the organ concerned, or something looks like a mouth. For example: "号，古，吗，和" and "可".

2.
   日字旁
   rìzìpáng

   用在字的上边、下边、左边、右边或中间都可以，常常用于左边。日字旁的字都与太阳、时间等意思有关。如："是、晋、明、旧、旬"。
   It can be placed at the top, bottom, left, right or center of a character, but usually on the left. Characters with "日" has the meaning of the sun, the time and so on. For example: "是，晋，明，旧" and "旬".

五　语 法 Grammar

（一）疑问句（4）：特指问句"哪儿""哪"

Interrogative sentences (4): Questions using the interrogative pronouns: *wh*-word

"哪儿"用来询问地点。如：
"哪儿" is used as an inquiry of a place. For example:

(1) A：你下午去哪儿？

　　B：我去图书馆。

(2) A：留学生食堂在哪儿？

　　B：在留学生宿舍的后边。

"哪"后面跟量词或数词加量词，表示要求在几个人或事物中确定一个。如：
"哪" is an interrogative word, which is followed by a measure word or a numeral-measure word phrase. It means to choose one from several persons or things. For example:

(1) A：哪位老师教汉语？

　　B：张老师教汉语。

(2) A：你是哪个班的学生？

　　B：我是二班的学生。

用疑问代词"什么、多少、几、谁、哪儿、哪"等来提问的句子，汉语称为特指问句，其语序跟陈述句一样，把陈述句中需要提问的部分改成疑问代词，就成了特指问句。如：
Questions with "什么, 多少, 几, 谁, 哪儿" and "哪" are questions using interrogative pronouns in Chinese. The word order of such a question is exactly the same as that of the declarative sentence. The question is formed by putting the *wh*-word in the position where the answer is located. For example:

(1) 我学习汉语。　　　　　　→　你学习什么？

(2) 我们学校有三千个学生。　→　你们学校有多少个学生？

(3) 他有三本中文书。　　　　→　他有几本中文书？

(4) 我们的汉语老师是张老师。→　你们的汉语老师是谁？

(5) 我去图书馆。　　　　　　→　你去哪儿？

(6) 王老师教口语。　　　　　→　哪位老师教口语？

注意：特指问句后面不能加"吗"。下面的说法是错误的：
Note: "吗" cannot be attached to the end of this kind of questions. The following sentences are not correct:

(1) *谁是你的汉语老师吗？

(2) *你去哪儿吗？

（二）定语和助词"的"　Attributives and the auxiliary word "的" (of)

句子中修饰或限制名词、名词性短语，表示人或事物的性状、数量、所属等的成分是定语。被修饰或限制的名词或名词短语叫"中心语"。定语一般都放在中心语前面。定语和中心语之间一般都可以加结构助词"的"。如：

A word or phrase which modifies or restricts a noun or a noun phrase, representing the nature, state, number and property of somebody or something, is called an attributive. The word or phrase modified by the attributive is called the head word. Usually, the attributive is placed before the head word. Generally, the structure particle "的" may be added between the attributive and the head word. For example:

(1) 他是这个学校的留学生。

(2) 那个白色的大楼是留学生食堂。

(3) 学校的图书馆很大。

1. 名词做定语时，如果这个名词是说明中心语性质的，一般不加"的"。如：

When a noun is used as an attributive, if the noun explains the property of the head word, "的" is not added.

日本人　　一本世界地图

2. 人称代词做定语表示领属关系时，如果中心语是亲属称谓或所属单位时，一般不加"的"。如：

When a personal pronoun is used as the attributive to represent the subordinative relation, if the head word is a family title or that of an organization, "的" is unnecessary to be added.

(1) 我爸爸是老师。

(2) 你姐姐也是留学生吗？

3. 数量结构做定语时，一般不加"的"。如：

When a numeral-measure word phrase is used as the attributive, "的" is usually not added. For example:

(1) 他家有五口人。

(2) 我们班有二十个同学。

4. 单音节形容词做定语一般不用"的"。如：

"的" is not used when a single-syllable adjective is the attributive. For example:

(1) 丁荣是我的好朋友。

(2) 他有一本新词典。

（三）形容词谓语句　Sentences with adjectival predicates

汉语中形容词可以直接做谓语。用形容词做谓语的句子叫形容词谓语句。形容词谓语句用来对事物进行描述和评价。

In Chinese, an adjective can be used as the predicate of a sentence independently, this kind of sentence is called a sentence of an adjective predicate. It is used to describe or evaluate something.

主语 + adj.	→	主语 + 不 + adj.
subject + adj.		subject + not + adj.
我很　　忙。	→	我　　　不　　忙。
她的汉语　很好。	→	她的汉语　不　　好。

一般的形容词谓语句，形容词前面要加副词。如：

In the sentence of adjective predicate, normally an adverb is placed before the adjective. For example:

(1) 这个汉字很难。

(2) 我们的口语老师很好。

如果不带副词，通常用于对举，句子的意思不再是描述和评价，而是带有比较的含义。如：

Without an adverb, an adjective is usually used in a parallel structure, and the sentence is not used for description or evaluation, but for comparison. For example:

这个汉字难，那个汉字不难。（比较）

注意：除了特殊强调外，形容词谓语句的主语与形容词之间不加"是"。一般不说：

Note: Except the special emphasis, "是" is not added between the subject and the adjective. The following sentences are not correct:

（1）＊发音是不难。

（2）＊天气是好。

六 》 重点词语 Key Words

语气词"吧"　　Modal particle "吧"

语气助词"吧"用在句尾，表示商量、提议、请求、同意等。课文中的句子"我们一起去吧"中的"吧"表示提议。

The modal particle "吧" appears at the end of a sentence to express consultation, proposal, request, approval and so on. The sentence "我们一起去吧" in the text means a proposal.

A：我们一起去吧。（请求、提议）

B：好吧。（同意）

七 》 练 习 Exercises

（一）朗读下面的短语　　Read the following phrases

走吧	来吧	去吧	不用谢	不用去	不用问
很远	不太远	比较远	中午好	下午好	晚上好
男同学	女老师	中文书	英文书	好朋友	新课本

汉语词典　　英文电影　　中国朋友　　留学生食堂

学生的书　　老师的书　　我的老师　　丁荣的词典

安达的书包　　老师的课本　　很难的汉字　　很好的老师

（二）替换练习　　Substitution

1. A：请问，留学生食堂在哪儿？
   B：留学生食堂在图书馆的后边。

   | 留学生宿舍 |
   | 教师宿舍 |
   | 那个楼 |
   | 教学楼 |

2. A：你去哪儿？
   B：我去留学生食堂。

   | 他 |
   | 王老师 |
   | 李明爱 |
   | 你们 |

3. A：哪位老师教语法？
   B：张老师教语法。

听力	王老师
口语	田老师
英语	李老师
法语	丁老师

（三）用"哪儿"或"哪"就画线部分提问　　Ask questions with "哪儿" "哪", according to the underlined part in each of the following sentences

1. 丁荣和波伟去教室。
2. 她是北京大学的留学生。
3. 留学生食堂在留学生宿舍的后边。
4. 田老师是三班的语法老师。
5. 下午他和朋友一起去图书馆。
6. 丁荣是英国人。

（四）选词填空 Choose and fill in the blanks

　　　　　吧　　看　　请问　　那儿　　不用

1. _____，图书馆在哪儿?

2. 下午没有课，我们一起去公园_____。

3. 你_____，留学生食堂在留学生宿舍的后边。

4. 你_____来我的宿舍，我去你的宿舍吧。

5. 我们的图书馆很好，我下午去_____学习。

（五）连词成句 Make sentences with the given words

1. 我　朋友　有　一个　新
   _____

2. 在　食堂　后边　图书馆　的
   _____

3. 老师　她　哥哥　是
   _____

4. 我们　吧　宿舍　回　一起
   _____

5. 哪个班　是　学生　的　她
   _____

6. 白色　留学生宿舍　是　大楼　那个　的
   _____

（六）找出需要加"的"的句子，并在适当的位置上加上"的" Find the sentences which are necessary to add "的", and then add "的" at the proper position to each of them

1. 他是一个很好老师。

2. 我有一本新词典。

3. 丁荣老师是张老师。

4. 这是我朋友汉语词典。

5. 我们学校有很多中国学生。

（七）改错句 Correct the following sentences

1. 你们学校有多少个留学生吗？

2. 我下午去我的朋友房间。

3. 今天下午你去哪？

4. 我的朋友是很好。

5. 你是一个哪国家人？

6. 李明爱是一个好的学生。

（八）用下列偏旁写出至少三个汉字 Write out at least three characters with the following radicals

口：_____   日：_____

（九）描写汉字 Trace the following characters

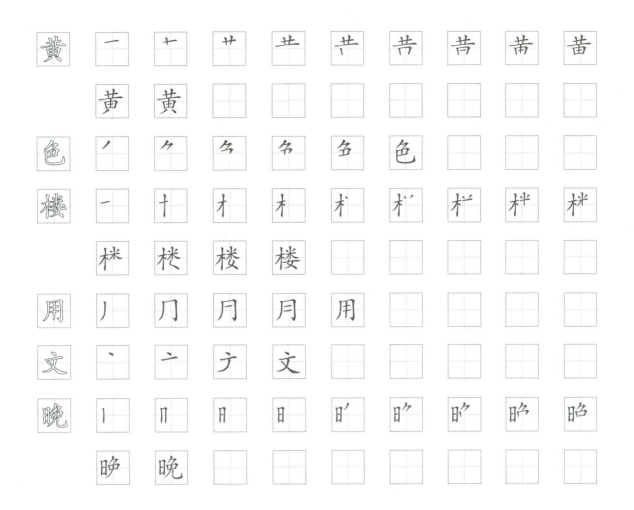

文化小贴士 Proverb

Yǒu zhì zhě, shì jìng chéng.
有志者，事竟成。

Where there is a will, there is a way.

第九课
没有课的时候，你做什么

Lesson 9

What do you do in your spare time

这一课你将学到

语法项目　Grammar

1. 概数的表达（1）：多（1）
   二十多节

2. 疑问句（5）：正反问句
   下午有没有课？

3. 称数法（2）：百以上的数字
   阅览室有三万多本中文书。

重点词语　Key Words

1. 介词"在"
   我在宿舍看书。

2. 名词"时候"
   没有课的时候，你做什么？

功能项目　Activity

询问数量（2）：询问百以上的数字

第九课 没有课的时候，你做什么

一 》生词 New Words

1.	时候	n.	shíhou	(duration of) time, period
2.	节	m.	jié	measure word for class, etc
3.	到	v.	dào	up until, up to
4.	阅览室	n.	yuèlǎnshì	reading room
5.	张	m.	zhāng	measure word for paper, beds, tables, mouth and face, etc
6.	桌子	n.	zhuōzi	table, desk
7.	百	num.	bǎi	hundred
8.	把	m.	bǎ	measure word for object with a handle
9.	椅子	n.	yǐzi	chair
10.	万	num.	wàn	ten thousand, large number
11.	千	num.	qiān	thousand
12.	外文	n.	wàiwén	foreign language
13.	种	m.	zhǒng	kind, sort, type
14.	报纸	n.	bàozhǐ	newspaper
15.	杂志	n.	zázhì	magazine, journal
16.	安静	adj.	ānjìng	quiet, peaceful, quietness
17.	干净	adj.	gānjìng	clean, neat
18.	这儿	pron.	zhèr	here

本课新字 New Characters

时	候	节	阅	览	张	桌
百	把	椅	万	千	种	报
纸	杂	志	安	静	干	净

二 课文 Texts

（一）没有课的时候，你做什么

A：你一个星期有多少节课？

B：二十多节。你一个星期有多少节课？

A：十多节。

B：你哪天有课？

A：星期一到星期五上午都有四节课。

B：下午有没有课？

A：星期一下午也有课。

B：没有课的时候你做什么？

A：我在宿舍看书。你做什么？

B：我去留学生阅览室。

A：留学生阅览室在哪儿？

B：在图书馆的二楼。

A：你今天下午去不去阅览室？

B：去，我们一起去吧。

（二）我们的留学生阅览室

今天下午没有课，我在留学生阅览室看书。阅览室在图书馆的二楼。我们的阅览室很大，有七十多张桌子，三百多把椅子。

阅览室有三万多本中文书、九千多本外文书、四十多种报纸和八十多种杂志。

留学生阅览室很安静，也很干净。很多留学生都喜欢在这儿看书。

三 汉字知识 About Chinese Characters

（一）怎样写好汉字（4）：突出笔画
Write characters beautifully (4): Highlight the main strokes

一个字中，往往有一笔是主要的，它对于整个字起着稳定和美化作用。把这一笔强调突出，写好了，字自然就平稳、富有神采。如：

There is often an important stroke in a character, which plays the role in balancing and beautifying the whole character. If this main stroke is written well and highlighted, the character becomes balanced, vivid and expressive.

以横为主笔的 horizontal is the main stroke：　言　英　主　最
以竖为主笔的 vertical is the main stroke：　年　千　丰　中
以撇为主笔的 throw is the main stroke：　　禾　在　多　有
以捺为主笔的 press is the main stroke：　　义　久　是　文　八
以钩为主笔的 J hook is the main stroke：　　龟　心　买　戎　也　凤

在汉字中也有不少偏旁部首做主笔的。如：
Some radicals are regarded as the main strokes. For example:

这　建　官　然

对于主笔，可以写得长一点儿，突出一点儿。我们在平时写汉字的时候，要逐步学会寻找主笔。

For a main stroke, it may be written a bit longer and heavier. One shall learn to find the main stroke in writing.

（二）偏旁：辶、口　Radicals: "辶" and "口"

1.
走之
zǒuzhī

用在字的左下角。走之旁的字都与行走等意义有关。如："进、远"。
Radical "辶" is usually placed at the left bottom of a character, represents the meaning of walk. For example: "进，远".

2.

国字框
guózìkuàng

用来把一个字包围起来，国字框的字都与围绕、环形、界限、约束等意义有关。如："国、回"。

This radical is used to surround a character. It implies the meaning of circling, surrounding, limit and restriction. For example: "国，回"。

四 语法 Grammar

（一）概数的表达（1）：多（1）
Expressions of approximate amounts (1)："多"(1)

"多"放在数词后，表示概数，意思是"超过，有零头"。"多"作为数词用法比较复杂。今天先学习其中一种用法。

"多" is placed after a numeral, meaning an approximate amount. As a numeral, the usage of "多" is complicated. One of the usages will be studied in this lesson.

数词为十位以上的整数，也就是说，数词的个位数为"零/0"时，如"三十、五百六十、四千七百"等，这时"多"表示整位数以下的零数。如："十多个"表示"十一、十二、十三或十四"等。

If the numbers are integers over ten, that is, the first digit is zero, such as "三十，五百六十，四千七百" etc, the word "多" indicates the remainder of the integers, e.g. the phrase "十多个" may mean "十一，十二，十三" or "十四" etc.

数词	+	多	+	量词	+	名词
number	+	多	+	measure word	+	noun
二十		多		位		老师
一百		多		个		人
三千		多		本		中文书

（二）疑问句（5）：正反问句
Interrogative sentences (5)：Affirmative-negative questions

把谓语主要成分的肯定式与否定式并列起来就构成正反问句。

123

The affirmative-negative question is a kind of interrogative sentence, formed by putting the affirmative and negative forms of the main elements of the predicate together.

主语	+	谓语	+	不	+	谓语	+	宾语
subject	+	predicate	+	不	+	predicate	+	object
汉语		难		不		难？		
她		是		不		是		留学生？
你		去		不		去		教室？

在口语里面，宾语也可以提前，放在"不"的前面。如：
In oral Chinese, the object can also be placed in front of "不". For example:

(1) 你去教室不去？

(2) 你是老师不是？

注意：动词"有"的否定式是"没有"。如：
Note: The negative form of the verb "有" is "没有". For example:

你今天有没有听力课？

（三）称数法（2）：百以上的数字
Reading of numbers (2) : Numbers over 100

汉语百以上的数字表达如下：
Numbers over 100 in Chinese can be expressed as the following:

一百零一……一百一十……一百六十………一百九十九………二百

二百零一……二百一十……二百六十………二百九十九………三百

三百零一………四百九十九……七百九十九………九百九十九………一千

一千零一…………………………………………………………一千九百九十九

一万零一………………………………………………………一万九千九百九十九

  307 读作：三百零七

  510 读作：五百一（十）

  80569 读作：八万零五百六十九

五 ▶ 重点词语 Key Words

（一）介词"在" Preposition "在"

介词"在"跟表示处所、方位的词语一起组成介词短语，做状语。放在动词前，表示动作发生的地点。如：

The preposition "在" combines with the word or phrase of locality into a prepositional phrase, acting the adverbial adjunct. It is placed before a verb, indicates the place where the action takes place. For example:

在	+	名词	+	动词	→	不在	+	名词	+	动词
在	+	noun	+	verb	→	不在	+	noun	+	verb
在		图书馆		学习	→	不在		图书馆		学习
在		商店		买东西	→	不在		商店		买东西

介词"在"的宾语一般是表示地点的词语。一个不表示地点的名词或代词，必须在后边加上"这儿"或"那儿"，才能做"在"的宾语，组成介词结构，修饰动词，表示处所。如：

The object of the preposition "在" is usually a word of locality. If it is not a noun or a preposition of locality, it must be followed by "这儿" "那儿" in the prepositional phrase. For example:

（1）我们在波伟那儿玩儿。

（2）他在朋友那儿吃饭。

（二）名词"时候" Noun "时候" (time, a period of time)

名词"时候"表示某一段时间或某一点时间。可以用在疑问句中询问时间。如：

The noun "时候" indicates a certain period of time or a certain time point. It can be used to inquire about time in a question. For example:

（1）A：你什么时候有课？

　　　B：我星期一、三、五上午和星期二下午有课。

（2）A：现在是什么时候？
　　　B：现在七点钟。

也可以用在陈述句中表示某一段时间或某一时间点。如：
It can also indicate a certain time or a certain period of time in a declarative sentence. For example:

不上课的时候，他在宿舍休息。

"……的时候"也可以省略为"……时"。如：
The expression "……的时候" can also be omitted as "……时". For example:

没有课时，他去图书馆学习。

六　练习　Exercises

（一）朗读下面的短语　Read the following phrases

中文书	中文报纸	外文书	外文杂志
一百七十	三百九十五	一千三百五十	九万四千三百二
八十多张	三百多位	五千多个	一万多本
二十五节课	五十七张桌子	八千五百本书	十种报纸
二十本杂志	三个阅览室	上课的时候	没有课的时候
去教室时	回宿舍时	在宿舍休息	在图书馆看书

（二）替换练习　Substitution

1. A：你们学校有多少个留学生？
　　B：我们学校有一千多个留学生。

学院（xuéyuàn, college）	二十
教室	一百
老师	五百
中国学生	一万五千

2. A：你回不回宿舍？
   B：我不回宿舍。

看	电影
去	教室
认识	她
学习	法语

3. 他在图书馆看书。

教室	上课
宿舍	学习
中国	学汉语
学校	工作

（三）读出下面的数字　Read out the following numbers

63　　105　　87　　531　　880　　1001　　19999　　64079

171　　340　　449　　700　　876　　34567　　30004　　76024

（四）填写合适的量词　Fill in the blanks with the proper measure words

一＿＿老师　　两＿＿学生　　三＿＿笔　　四＿＿书

五＿＿书包　　六＿＿桌子　　七＿＿人　　十一＿＿苹果

九＿＿椅子　　十＿＿杂志　　八＿＿课　　十二＿＿国家

（五）把下面的一般疑问句改成正反问句　Turn the following sentences into affirmative-negative questions

1. 你是留学生吗？

2. 你的宿舍安静吗？

3. 今天下午你去图书馆吗？

4. 你有哥哥吗？

5. 留学生食堂在留学生宿舍的后边吗？

6. 丁荣是你的好朋友吗？

7．明天上午你有听力课吗？

8．你们的教室远吗？

（六）连词成句 Make sentences with the given words

1．我们　有　一万多个　学生　学校
　　_____

2．她　课　星期五　没有　下午
　　_____

3．我　看书　喜欢　图书馆　在
　　_____

4．你　明天　下午　有　汉语课　没有
　　_____

5．图书馆　九万　有　中文书　本　多
　　_____

6．我的　很安静　也　宿舍　很干净
　　_____

7．是　她的　哥哥　不是　老师
　　_____

（七）改错句 Correct the following sentences

1．没有课时候，你什么做？

2．我一个星期有二十五个课。

3．这个学校有三万多五千个中国学生。

4．他学习汉语在教室。

5．我星期一也下午有三节课。

6．她喜欢在阅览室不看书。

(八) 用下列偏旁写出至少三个汉字 Write out at least three characters with the following radicals

辶：_____   口（国字框）：_____

(九) 描写汉字 Trace the following characters

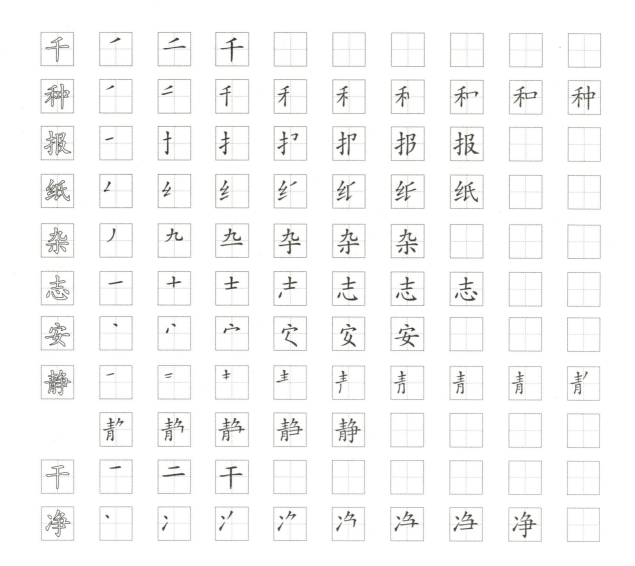

文化小贴士 Proverb

Xué ér shí xí zhī, bú yì yuè hū?
学而时习之，不亦说乎？

Is it not pleasant to learn with a constant perseverance and application?

第十课 复习（二）

Lesson 10 Review (II)

一 》 生 词 New Words

1.	爸爸	n.	bàba	dad
2.	妈妈	n.	māma	mum
3.	哥哥	n.	gēge	elder brother
4.	妹妹	n.	mèimei	younger sister
5.	照片儿	n.	zhàopiānr	photograph, picture
6.	公司	n.	gōngsī	company
7.	经理	n.	jīnglǐ	manager
8.	常常	adv.	chángcháng	frequently, usually, often
9.	晚	adj.	wǎn	late
10.	商店	n.	shāngdiàn	store, shop
11.	售货员	n.	shòuhuòyuán	shop assistant, salesclerk
12.	中间	n.	zhōngjiān	middle

131

13.	努力	adj.	nǔlì	hard, hard-working
14.	左边	n.	zuǒbian	left, the left side
15.	画	v.	huà	draw, paint
16.	画儿	n.	huàr	drawing, painting, picture
17.	右边	n.	yòubian	the right side
18.	周	n.	zhōu	week
19.	有意思		yǒu yìsi	interesting, fascinating

本课新字 New Characters

照 片 常 商 店 售 货
间 努 左 画 右 意 思

二 课文 Text

我家有五口人

Wǒ jiào Lǐ Míng'ài, shì Hánguórén. Wǒ jiā yǒu wǔ kǒu rén: bàba、māma、
我叫李明爱，是韩国人。我家有五口人：爸爸、妈妈、

gēge、mèimei hé wǒ. Zhè shì wǒmen jiā de zhàopiānr. Nǐ kàn, zhè shì wǒ de
哥哥、妹妹和我。这是我们家的照片儿。你看，这是我的

bàba māma. Wǒ bàba shì yì jiā gōngsī de jīnglǐ, tāmen gōngsī hěn dà, yǒu
爸爸妈妈。我爸爸是一家公司的经理，他们公司很大，有

yìqiān duō ge zhíyuán. Bàba gōngzuò hěn máng, chángcháng hěn wǎn huí jiā. Mā
一千多个职员。爸爸工作很忙，常常很晚回家。妈

ma shì shāngdiàn de shòuhuòyuán, tā gōngzuò bú tài máng.
妈是商店的售货员，她工作不太忙。

爸爸妈妈的后边是哥哥、妹妹和我。中间的是我哥哥,他在美国学习英语,他学习很努力。哥哥的左边是我妹妹,妹妹在韩国,她很喜欢画画儿。哥哥右边的这个人是我。我在中国学习汉语,我们一周有二十多节课。汉语很有意思,我喜欢汉语。

三 练习 Exercises

(一) 根据课文内容判断正误 Judge the following sentences true or false according to the text

1. 李明爱家有爸爸、妈妈、姐姐、弟弟和她。　　　　(　　)

2. 照片儿上爸爸和妈妈在前边。　　　　　　　　　　(　　)

3. 妈妈是商店的售货员,工作很忙。　　　　　　　　(　　)

4. 李明爱学习汉语,妹妹学习英语。　　　　　　　　(　　)

5. 李明爱的哥哥喜欢画画儿。　　　　　　　　　（　）

6. 李明爱觉得汉语很有意思。　　　　　　　　　（　）

（二）选词填空　Fill in the blanks with the given words

中间　　常常　　有意思　　努力　　周　　照片儿

1. 我有五张家人的_____。

2. 哥哥在_____，我在左边，弟弟在右边。

3. 我一_____有三个下午有课。

4. 一年级二班的学生学习都很_____。

5. 没有课的时候，丁荣_____去留学生阅览室。

6. 这本英文杂志很_____。

（三）把括号里的词填入适当的位置　Put the words in the parentheses at the proper positions

1. A 这本 B 是汉语书，那本 C 是 D 汉语书。　　（也）

2. 他 A 学习汉语，B 他的朋友们 C 也 D 学习汉语。（都）

3. 我们 A 学校 B 有一千五百 C 名 D 留学生。　　（多）

4. 我 A 常常 B 和朋友 C 去公园 D 玩儿。　　　　（一起）

5. 我 A 姐姐 B 朋友 C 都是英国 D 人。　　　　　（的）

6. 她 A 喜欢 B 留学生 C 阅览室 D 看书。　　　　（在）

7. A 我 B 和朋友一起 C 去 D 食堂吃饭。　　　　（常常）

（四）根据画线部分用疑问代词提问　Ask questions according to the underlined part of each sentence with an interrogative pronoun

1. 波伟是<u>安达</u>的同学。

2. 姐姐有<u>四</u>个中国朋友。

3. 她是<u>二</u>班的汉语老师。

4. 这是一本<u>汉语</u>书。

5．丁荣常常和波伟一起去图书馆。

6．我下午去图书馆。

7．他们班有二十一位同学。

8．他有一本汉语词典。

(五) 连词成句　Make sentences with the given words

1．汉语　老师　谁　你们　是　的

2．学生　他　是　我们班　也　的

3．是　姐姐　一个　很努力　学生　的

4．常常　我爸爸　回家　很晚

5．学习　她　教室　在　喜欢

6．前边　食堂　留学生　图书馆　在　的

7．八百多　他们　有　学校　留学生　个

8．多少　你们班　男同学　有　个

(六) 改错句　Correct the following sentences

1．我有一个汉语词典。

2．谁是你们的汉语老师吗？

3．他的汉语书是很新。

4．波伟星期二下午有上课。

5．张老师是很好老师。

6．我爸爸是经理，哥哥姐姐都也是经理。

7．这是留学生的办公室吗？

8．她家有人三口。

（七）用下列偏旁写出至少三个汉字　Write out at least three characters with the following radicals

女：_____　　　讠：_____

亻：_____　　　宀：_____

日：_____　　　口：_____

辶：_____　　　囗：_____

（八）写作　Writings

选择下面的词语写一段话，介绍你的学校和班级（字数不少于80字）。
Write a short passage by choosing the following words to introduce your school and class (at least 80 characters).

| 学生 | 图书馆 | 食堂 | 教室 | 宿舍 | 旁边 | 前边 |
| 认识 | 努力 | 朋友 | 在 | 多 | 也 | 都 | 好 |

（九）描写汉字　Trace the following characters

片	丿	丿	片	片
常	丶	丷	丷	屮	屮	常	常	常
常	常
商	丶	亠	六	产	产	商	商	商
商	商
店	丶	亠	广	广	庄	庄	店	店
售	丿	亻	亻	亻	乍	隹	隹	隹
售	售
货	丿	亻	亻	化	货	货	货
间	丶	丨	门	门	间	间	间
努	乚	夕	女	奴	奴	努	努
左	一	ナ	ナ	左	左
画	一	一	丅	画	面	画	画
右	一	ナ	ナ	右	右

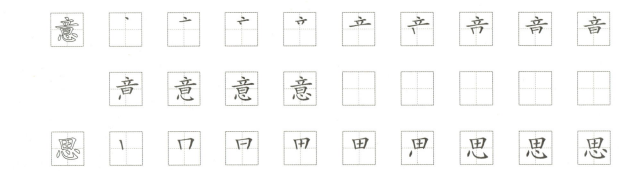

文化小贴士 Proverb

Yè jīng yú qín, huāng yú xī.
业精于勤，荒于嬉。

Knowledge can be obtained through diligence, and may be neglected because of playing.

第十一课
一斤多少钱

Lesson

How much one jin

这一课你将学到

语法项目　Grammar

1. 疑问句（6）：选择问句"A 还是 B"
   你喜欢吃苹果还是橘子？

2. "的"字结构
   红的

3. 人民币的表示法：元（块）、角（毛）、分
   二十三元五角

4. 双宾语句
   我给售货员二十五元钱。

重点词语　Key Words

1. 量词"（一）点儿"
   我们买一点儿水果吧。

2. 副词"一共"
   一共多少钱？

功能项目　Activity

付款

一 生词 New Words

1.	斤	m.	jīn	of weight (equal to 1/2 kilogram)
2.	钱	n.	qián	money
3.	（一）点儿	n.	(yì) diǎnr	a little, some (for things that are not countable)
4.	水果	n.	shuǐguǒ	fruit
5.	苹果	n.	píngguǒ	apple
6.	还是	conj.	háishi	or
7.	橘子	n.	júzi	orange
8.	要	v.	yào	want, ask for, demand
9.	红	adj.	hóng	red
10.	块	m.	kuài	*yuan*, for money
11.	毛	m.	máo	unit of fractional RMB, ten cents
12.	再	adv.	zài	again, more
13.	西瓜	n.	xīguā	watermelon
14.	半	num.	bàn	half
15.	一共	adv.	yígòng	altogether, in all
16.	怎么	pron.	zěnme	how
17.	付	v.	fù	pay for
18.	微信	n.	wēixìn	WeChat
19.	支付宝	n.	zhīfùbǎo	Alipay
20.	扫码		sǎo mǎ	scan a QR code
21.	超市	n.	chāoshì	supermarket
22.	饼干	n.	bǐnggān	biscuit, cookie
23.	牛奶	n.	niúnǎi	milk
24.	瓶	n.	píng	bottle
25.	给	v.	gěi	give
26.	找	v.	zhǎo	give change
27.	元	m.	yuán	unit of fractional RMB
28.	角	m.	jiǎo	unit of fractional RMB, ten cents

本课新字 New Characters

斤	钱	点	还	橘	要	块	毛	瓜
半	共	微	付	市	给	找	元	角

二 课文 Texts

（一）一斤多少钱

丁荣： 李明爱，我们买一点儿水果吧。你喜欢吃苹果还是橘子？

李明爱： 我喜欢吃苹果。

丁荣： 我们买点儿苹果。一斤多少钱？

售货员： 你们要红的还是要黄的？

丁荣： 红的好，要红的吧。

售货员： 一斤九块五毛钱，你们要多少？

丁荣： 要三斤。

售货员： 好，三斤红苹果，二十八块五。

李明爱： 再买个西瓜吧。多少钱一斤？

售货员：四块六一斤，要大的还是要小的？

李明爱：我们两个人吃，要个小的吧。

售货员：这个西瓜四斤半，二十块七。

丁荣：一共多少钱？

售货员：苹果二十八块五毛，西瓜二十块七，一共四十九块两毛钱。

丁荣：怎么付？微信还是支付宝？

售货员：微信吧！请扫码。

（二）一共二十三元五角

今天下午，天气很好，我们没有课，我和李明爱一起去超市买东西。她买饼干，我买面包和牛奶。一包饼干八元钱，一个面包九元五角，一瓶牛奶六元钱。一共二十三元五角。我给售货员二十五元，她找我一元五角。

三 注 释 Note

一斤多少钱？ How much one *jin*?

询问价钱时可以说"一斤多少钱"，也可以说"多少钱一斤"。
To ask for the price, one may say "一斤多少钱" or "多少钱一斤".

四 汉字知识 About Chinese Characters

（一）怎样写好汉字（5）：主次分明
Write characters beautifully (5) : The main strokes must be clear

为了突出主笔，有些笔画就要稍稍收缩一点儿，以免喧宾夺主，比如"文"的主笔是"㇏"，所以"丿"就不能写得比"㇏"长，如"文"。"然"的主笔是"灬"，所以"然"就不能写成"然"。

To highlight the main stroke, some strokes must be shrunk so as not to shadow the main stroke. For example, in "文", the press stroke is a main stroke, therefore, the throw stroke cannot be longer than the press stroke. As for the main stroke in "然" is "灬", so "然" cannot be written as "然".

由几部分组成的合体字，大多数都有主次之分，或大或小，或宽或窄，要注意掌握比例，有所突出，不能平分秋色。如：

Most multi-component characters consist of primary and secondary strokes, such as big or small, wide or narrow. One must learn how to divide the proportion so as to highlight the main strokes, instead of paying equal attention to them. For example:

以右边为主的 main stroke on the right：　拜　统　除
以左边为主的 main stroke on the left：　　邻　却　劲
以上边为主的 main stroke at the top：　　春　奔　赏
以下边为主的 main stroke at the bottom：　朵　紧　聚

143

合体字之间除了主次有别外，还要注意不能把一个汉字写得分了家。如：

In addition to the main strokes, a multi-component character cannot be written as two independent ones. For example:

林　不能写成：木木
烧　不能写成：火尧
放　不能写成：方攵

主笔虽然应该强调、突出，但也不能过分。如：

The main stroke must be emphasized and highlighted, but not be overemphasized. For example:

大　不能写成：大
中　不能写成：中
主　不能写成：主

（二）偏旁：艹、氵　Radicals: "艹" and "氵"

1. **艹** 草字头 cǎozìtóu
   用在字的上边。带草字头的字都与植物等意义有关。如："茶、苹"。
   Radical "艹" is placed at the top of a character, meaning plants, such as "茶，苹".

2. **氵** 三点水 sāndiǎnshuǐ
   用在字的左边，带三点水的字都与水流等意义有关。如"江、汉、河"。
   This radical is placed on the left of a character, meaning water, such as "江，汉，河".

五　语法 Grammar

（一）疑问句（6）：选择疑问句"A 还是 B"
Interrogative sentences (6): Alternative questions "A 还是 B"

选择疑问句是问话者提供两种或两种以上的情况供回答者选择回答的疑问句。其句型为：

Questions in which two or more choices are paralleled for the answerer to choose. The pattern is:

问：　A 还是 B？　　　　　　　→　　答：A（/B）。
　　　A　or　B?　　　　　　　　　　　　A（/B）。

你学习中文还是学习英文？　　→　　我学习中文。/ 我学习英文。

她是美国人还是德国人？　　　→　　她是美国人。/ 她是德国人。

（二）"的"字结构　　的-phrase

"的"字结构是由"的"字附加在名词、代词、形容词、动词等实词或短语后面组成的，它的作用相当于名词，可以在句中充当主语、宾语。如：

The 的-phrase is one in which "的" is attached to a notional word or phrase, such as a noun, pronoun, adjective, verb, and so on. The 的-phrase functions as a noun and acts as the subject and the object. For example:

(1) 我的笔很新，哥哥的很旧。　　（我的笔很新，哥哥的笔很旧。）

(2) 这本是我的，那本是他的。　　（这本是我的书，那本是他的书。）

(3) 这辆红色的很便宜。　　　　　（这辆红色的自行车很便宜。）

(4) 我们去买点儿吃的吧。　　　　（我们去买点儿吃的东西吧。）

（三）人民币的表示法　　Expressions of Renminbi (CNY)

人民币的单位从大到小有：元、角、分，在口语里可以说：块、毛、分。如：

There are *yuan*, *jiao* and *fen* in CNY. In oral Chinese, they are replaced by *kuai*, *mao* and *fen*. For example:

3.54 元	读成：三元五角四分	或	三块五毛四分
4.3 元	读成：四元三角	或	四块三毛
640 元	读成：六百四十元	或	六百四十块
3.05 元	读成：三元零五分	或	三块零五分
0.45 元	读成：四角五分	或	四毛五分
100.60 元	读成：一百元零六角	或	一百块零六毛

在口语当中最后一位的单位可以省略。如：
In oral Chinese, the last unit can be omitted.

3.54 元　　也可读成：　　三块五毛四
4.3 元　　 也可读成：　　四块三
640 元　　 也可读成：　　六百四
0.45 元　　也可读成：　　四毛五

（四）双宾语句　Sentences with double objects

汉语有些动词可以带两个宾语：第一个叫间接宾语，一般指人；第二个叫直接宾语，一般指事物。如：

Some verbs in Chinese can have two objects. The first one is called an indirect object, which refers to a person, while the second one is a direct object, which refers to a thing. For example:

(1) 我给售货员一百块钱。

(2) 售货员找我七十五块五毛。

但汉语里能带双宾语的动词比较少，常见的可以带双宾语的动词有："教、给、借、还、问、回答、告诉"等。如：

However, only a few verbs can have double objects, such as: "教，给，借，还，问，回答" and "告诉". For example:

(1) 张老师教我们语法。

(2) 爸爸给我一百块钱。

六　重点词语 Key Words

（一）量词"（一）点儿"　Measure word "（一）点儿"

量词"（一）点儿"表示少量，也可以省略为"点儿"。如：

"点儿" is a measure word, representing a small quantity, and it is the short form of "一点儿". For example:

动词	+	（一）点儿	+	宾语
verb	+	（一）点儿	+	object
买		（一）点儿		水果
喝		（一）点儿		水
吃		（一）点儿		东西

（二）副词"一共" Adverb "一共"

副词"一共"表示合在一起，宾语通常是数量词组。如：

The adverb "一共" means to put together. Its object is often a numeral-measure word phrase. For example:

(1) 三个班一共是四十五人。

(2) 她一共有二百多块钱。

有时候，"一共"可以直接修饰数量短语。如：

Sometimes, the numeral-measure word can be added to "一共" directly. For example:

A：一共（是）多少钱？

B：一共（是）二十五块五毛钱。

七 练习 Exercises

（一）朗读下面的短语 Read the following phrases

三块五毛六	九十九块六毛	一千零五块	一万五千块
买书包	买课本	买点儿什么	来点儿苹果
找我钱	给她词典	教我们语法	教留学生汉语
一共是二十块	一共有一百本	一共二十斤	一共五十个
多少钱	多少斤	五斤半	十斤半
爸爸的	妈妈的	他们的	我们的
红色的	便宜的	吃的	用的

（二）替换练习　Substitution

1. A：我买<u>苹果</u>，多少钱<u>一斤</u>？
   B：<u>十块</u>。

笔	一支	三块五
本子	一个	五块
咖啡（kāfēi, coffee）	一杯（bēi, cup）	四十五块
书包	一个	八十八块

2. A：你要几<u>斤</u><u>苹果</u>？
   B：我要<u>六斤</u>。

个	西瓜	一
支	笔	三
个	本子	五
本	汉语书	七

3. A：你要<u>大</u>的还是要<u>小</u>的？
   B：我要<u>小</u>的。

苹果	西瓜
白的	黑的
新的	旧的
便宜的	贵的

4. 我<u>给</u> <u>售货员</u> <u>一百块钱</u>。

给	弟弟	一件衣服
教	他	英语
找	她	五十五块钱
给	姐姐	一本词典

（三）读出下面的钱数　Read out the following numbers

| 0.11 | 8.00 | 9.50 | 0.03 | 450.70 | 300.05 | 1109.36 | 3600.00 |
| 6.43 | 10.00 | 56.66 | 70.18 | 678.40 | 1111.55 | 80001.00 | 94507.95 |

(四)用"还是"提问　Ask questions with "还是"

1．苹果　　　　西瓜　　　　2．教室　　　　超市

3．中国人　　　韩国人　　　4．汉语　　　　英语

5．上午　　　　下午　　　　6．黑色　　　　红色

7．汉英词典　　英汉词典　　8．张老师　　　王老师

(五)按照例句改写句子　Rewrite the following sentences after the model

例：这是我的书。　　→ 这本书是我的。

1．这是妹妹的苹果。　→ _____。

2．这是一本英文词典。　→ _____。

3．这是一支蓝色的笔。　→ _____。

4．这是一个新书包。　→ _____。

5．这是妹妹的衣服。　→ _____。

(六)连词成句　Make sentences with the given words

1．口语　教　张老师　他们

_____

2．本子　五毛钱　三个　一共　十三块

_____

3．法语　王明　英语　学习　还是

_____

4．吃　你　还是　饼干　面包

_____

5．是　中文的　晚上的电影　英文的　还是

_____

6. 牛奶 给我 哥哥 面包 一个 和 一瓶

_____

（七）改错句 Correct the following sentences

1. 我给一百块钱售货员。

2. 汉语是难是不难？

3. 张老师我们教听力。

4. 你要苹果还是香蕉吗？

5. 我找两元五角他。

6. 我有两个苹果，你要大还是要小？

（八）用下列偏旁写出至少三个汉字 Write out at least three characters with the following radicals

艹：_____　　　氵：_____

（九）描写汉字 Trace the following characters

第十一课 一斤多少钱

文化小贴士 Proverb

Hǎinèi cún zhījǐ, tiānyá ruò bǐlín.
海内存知己，天涯若比邻。

As long as one had a true friend, they are close even when far away.

第十二课
你的生日是什么时候

Lesson 12
When is your birthday

语法项目　Grammar

1. 日期表达法：年、月、日
   二零一零年九月三十日

2. 疑问句（7）：语调疑问句
   你的生日是九月三十号？

3. 名词谓语句
   今天九月三十日。

4. 状语（2）：时间状语和地点状语
   晚上六点在我的房间举行生日晚会。

重点词语　Key Words

1. 介词"给"
   早上爸爸妈妈给我打电话，祝我生日快乐。

2. 后缀"们"
   朋友们

功能项目　Activity
询问日期

一 生词 New Words

1.	号	n.	hào	date, number
2.	举行	v.	jǔxíng	hold (a meeting, contest, etc.), perform, give
3.	晚会	n.	wǎnhuì	evening party
4.	蛋糕	n.	dàngāo	cake
5.	啤酒	n.	píjiǔ	beer
6.	饮料	n.	yǐnliào	drink
7.	点	n.	diǎn	o'clock
8.	日	n.	rì	day
9.	打	v.	dǎ	call, make (a telephone call)
10.	电话	n.	diànhuà	telephone, phone call
11.	祝	v.	zhù	express good wishes, wish
12.	快乐	adj.	kuàilè	happy, joyful, cheerful
13.	送	v.	sòng	give, deliver
14.	礼物	n.	lǐwù	gift, present
15.	唱	v.	chàng	sing
16.	歌	n.	gē	song
17.	跳舞		tiào wǔ	dance

本课新字 New Characters

号 举 行 会 蛋 糕 啤
酒 饮 点 打 话 祝 快
送 礼 物 唱 歌 跳 舞

二 课文 Texts

（一）你的生日是什么时候

Lǐ Míng'ài: Wáng Míng, Nǐ nǎ nián chūshēng de?
李明爱：王明，你哪年出生的？

Wáng Míng: Èrlínglíngyī nián.
王 明：二零零一年。

Lǐ Míng'ài: Nǐ de shēngrì shì shénme shíhou?
李明爱：你的生日是什么时候？

Wáng Míng: Wǒ de shēngrì shì jiǔyuè sānshí hào.
王 明：我的生日是九月三十号。

Lǐ Míng'ài: Nǐ de shēngrì shì jiǔyuè sānshí hào? Wǒ de yě shì.
李明爱：你的生日是九月三十号？我的也是。

Wáng Míng: Shì ma? Míngtiān shì jiǔyuè sānshí hào, wǒmen yìqǐ jǔxíng ge shēngrì wǎnhuì ba!
王 明：是吗？明天是九月三十号，我们一起举行个生日晚会吧！

Lǐ Míng'ài: Hǎo! wǒ de fángjiān bǐjiào dà, zài wǒ de fángjiān jǔxíng ba.
李明爱：好！我的房间比较大，在我的房间举行吧。

Wáng Míng: Míngtiān xīngqī jǐ?
王 明：明天星期几？

Lǐ Míng'ài: Xīngqīliù, wǒmen méiyǒu kè, yìqǐ qù chāoshì ba, mǎi diǎnr chī de、hē de.
李明爱：星期六，我们没有课，一起去超市吧，买点儿吃的、喝的。

Wáng Míng: Hǎo, wǒmen mǎi yí ge dàngāo, mǎi yìdiǎnr shuǐguǒ, zài mǎi diǎnr píjiǔ、yǐnliào.
王 明：好，我们买一个蛋糕，买一点儿水果，再买点儿啤酒、饮料。

李明爱：明天我们几点去超市？

王明：下午一点半吧。

李明爱：好，明天见！

（二）今天是我的生日

我二零零一年九月三十日出生，今天九月三十日，是我的生日。早上爸爸妈妈给我打电话，祝我生日快乐。晚上六点在我的房间举行生日晚会，朋友们都来我房间，祝我生日快乐，他们送我很多生日礼物。我们一起唱歌、跳舞。这是一个很有意思的生日晚会。

三 注释 Notes

（一）你哪年出生的？ In which year were you born?

"的"是强调格式"是……的"省略形式，肯定句中，"是"可以省略，这个结构用来表示强调，本句强调已完成动作的时间。

The word "的" is the omitted form of the emphasis structure "是……的". In an affirmative sentence, "是" can be omitted. This structure is used to emphasize. In the above example, it emphasizes the time of a completed action.

（二）是吗？ Is that so?

"是吗"表示惊讶、惊喜等语气。

"是吗" expresses the mood of surprising or astonishing.

（三）我们一起举行个生日晚会吧！ Let's have a birthday party together!

如果量词前面的数词为"一"，数词"一"通常可以省略。如：

If the number "一" is before a measure word, it can be omitted. For example:

(1) 你吃（一）个苹果吧！

(2) 我们去买个蛋糕吧！

（四）明天见。 See you tomorrow.

告别的时候，可以用下次见面的时间来表示。如：

At the moment of departure, one may suggest the next time to meet. For example:

一会儿见　　　　　　　　明天见

八点见　　　　　　　　　下星期见

四 汉字知识　About Chinese Characters

（一）怎样写好汉字（6）：点画呼应
Write characters beautifully (6)：Responding of dots and strokes

汉字手写体的行楷和印刷体不一样。手写体的行楷虽然每一笔不相连，但前一笔和后一笔，形虽断而意相连，点画之间有所呼应。如：

Running hand of Chinese characters is different from its printing type. Each stroke does not connect to the other, but two neighbour strokes give the hint of connection even if they look like separated, for the dots and the strokes in a character respond to each other. For example:

火：火　　　　兴：兴　　　　法：法

这样，既可使互不相干的单调的点画联系起来，使字变得美观；又能提高书写速度，节省时间。在点画呼应的基础上，字写得熟练了，有些笔画还可以连写。如：

Therefore, the connection between two separated strokes makes a character look beautiful, and one can write quickly and save the time. On the bases of the responding between the dots and strokes, with enough practice, one can write some strokes connected. For example:

红：红　　　　这：这　　　　欢：欢　　　　转：转

实际上，每个中国人写字都不是一笔一画都分得很清楚的，有些笔画总是连着写的。不过这是学习书写较高阶段的事了。

In fact, when a Chinese writes a character, he may not write every stroke clearly, and some strokes are always written together.

（二）偏旁：纟、八　Radicals: "纟" and "八"

1. 纟
绞丝旁
jiǎosīpáng

用在字的左边，绞丝旁取"丝"字的半边，绞丝旁的字一般与丝织品或纺织活动有关。如："红、绿"。

"纟" is used on the left side of a character. It is the half of the character "丝". Characters with this radical are generally related to silk or the weaving activity. For example: "红，绿".

2. 用在字上边或下边，八字旁的字都与分开等意义有关。如："公、共"。
Radical "八" is placed at the top or bottom, meaning departing. For example: "公, 共".

五 语法 Grammar

（一）日期表达法　Expression of date

汉语里日期的表达顺序是由大到小的：年、月、日。如：
The correct order of date in Chinese is: year, month, day. For example:

(1) 一九九八年十一月十二日

(2) 二零二一年五月三十日

表达日期、星期等时间，可以用名词谓语句，也可以用"是"字句。如：
To express the date and day of week, the sentence with nominal predicates can be used, so is 是-structure. For example:

(1) 今天九月三十日。/ 今天是九月三十日。

(2) 昨天星期二。/ 昨天是星期二。

（二）疑问句（7）：语调疑问句

Interrogative sentences (7)：Tone interrogative sentences

陈述句带上疑问语调也可以直接构成一个疑问句，这样的问句称为语调疑问句。如：
When a declarative sentence is uttered in an interrogative tone, it changes into an interrogative one, which is called tone interrogative sentence. For example:

(1) 明天是你的生日？

(2) 你也是这个学校的学生？

与一般疑问句相比，语调疑问句带有惊讶的语气，而一般疑问句只表示疑问。如：
The tone interrogative sentence has the tone of surprise, while the general interrogative sentence is only to ask a question. For example:

(1) 你是中国人吗？（只是疑问）

(2) 你是中国人？（除疑问外，还有惊讶的语气）

（三）名词谓语句 Sentences with nominal predicates

名词谓语句是名词、名词短语、数量词、时间词等做谓语的句子。名词谓语句常用来表示时间、价格、日期、数量、天气、年龄、籍贯等。名词谓语句意思是"S 是 N"，但谓语前不用"是"。

A sentence with a nominal predicate is one, in which the predicate is a noun, nominal phrase, numeral-measure word and the noun of time. It is often used to express time, price, date, amount, weather, age and native place, etc. It means that "S is N", but there is no "是" before the predicate (Noun).

主语 + 谓语	→	主语 + 不是 + 谓语
subject + predicate	→	subject + be not + predicate
今天　九月三十日	→	今天　不是　九月三十日
今天　星期一	→	今天　不是　星期一
我　　南京人	→	我　　不是　南京人

（四）状语（2）：时间状语和地点状语
Adverbial adjuncts (2) : Adverbial adjuncts of time and locality

时间词充当的状语叫时间状语，时间状语表示动作发生的时间。时间状语可以在谓语的前面，也可以在主语的前面。如：

The time nouns acting the adverbial in a sentence is called the adverbial adjunct of time expressing the time when an action takes place. It can be placed before the predicate or before the subject. For example:

我们明天上午没有课。(明天上午我们没有课。)

表示地点的状语叫地点状语，说明在什么地方做什么事情。地点状语放在谓语的前面。

The adverbial adjunct of locality explains the place where an action occurs. Usually, It is placed before the predicate. For example:

（1）他在这个学校学习汉语。

（2）在外面吃饭。

如果时间状语和地点状语同时出现，时间状语要放在地点状语的前面。如：

If adverbial adjuncts of time and locality exist in the same sentence, the adverbial adjunct of time is before that of locality. For example:

（1）我们早上八点二十在宿舍楼门口见吧。

（2）晚上六点我在家里举行生日晚会。

六 重点词语 Key Words

（一）介词"给" Preposition "给"

介词"给"同名词、代词组成介词短语，做状语，表示动作的对象或受益者。如：

Preposition "给" can form a prepositional phrase with a noun or pronoun, indicating the object of the action. For example:

给	+	名词/代词	+	动词
给	+	noun/pronoun	+	verb
给		你们		介绍一下儿
给		朋友		写信
给		爸爸妈妈		打电话

(二)后缀"们" Suffix of "们"

"们"是一个后缀,用在代词后面,表示复数,如"我们""你们""他们"。也可以放在指人的名词后面表示复数。如:"同学们、老师们、朋友们"。

"们" is a suffix, which is used after a pronoun, signing the plural number, e.g. "我们""你们" and "他们". It can also be placed after a noun of personal reference. For example: "同学们""老师们" and "朋友们".

注意:名词前有数量词时,后面不能加"们"。下面的说法是错误的:

Note: If numeral-measure word phrase exist before a noun, "们" cannot be added. The following sentences are not correct:

* 三位老师们

* 十五个同学们

七 练 习 Exercises

(一)朗读下面的短语 Read the following phrases

喜欢唱歌	喜欢跳舞	举行晚会
朋友们	老师们	学生们
买本书	要个西瓜	买瓶饮料
打个电话	吃个苹果	送个礼物
天气很好	今天十月一号	明天不是星期六
一九九八年一月三日	二零零年十二月十二号	二零二零年八月十五号
祝你生日快乐	祝你圣诞(Shèngdàn)快乐	祝你新年快乐
给爸爸打电话	给你介绍一下	给朋友写(xiě)信
送我一件衣服	送爸爸一本书	送朋友一支笔

（二）替换练习　Substitution

1. A：你哪年出生的？
   B：我 2008 年出生的。

爸爸	1967 年
妈妈	1979 年
王老师	1988 年
丁荣	2002 年

2. A：你的生日是什么时候？
   B：十一月十一号。

圣诞节	十二月二十五号
新年	一月一号
姐姐的生日	十月十号
爸爸的生日	三月十六日

3. A：九月三十号星期几？
   B：九月三十号星期六。

你的生日	星期六
十月一号	星期一
这个月六号	星期四
今年圣诞节	星期五

4. A：祝你生日快乐！
   B：谢谢。

   新年快乐
   圣诞快乐
   天天快乐
   身体健康（jiànkāng, healthy）

（三）读出下面的年月日　Read out the following dates

1894. 7. 1	1947. 8. 10	1951. 4. 11
1978. 10. 10	1987. 1. 15	1996. 9. 6
2000. 5. 26	2009. 3. 26	2022. 8. 31

（四）选词填空　Choose and fill in the blanks

号　　举行　　点　　送　　礼物　　给

1. 我常常 _____ 朋友们打电话。

2. 现在是上午十 _____。

3. 这本书是给你的生日 _____。

4. 姐姐 _____ 她一件漂亮的衣服。

5. 今天的晚会在哪儿 _____ ？

6. 今天是九月三十 _____。

（五）连词成句　Make sentences with the given words

1. 星期天　我　学习　汉语　在图书馆
   _____

2. 吧　我们　去公园　明天　一起
   _____

3. 是　今天　不　星期一
   _____

4. 我　给妈妈　打　晚上　电话
   _____

5. 礼物　送我　朋友们　生日　很多
   _____

（六）改错句　Correct the following sentences

1. 今天星期五，不星期六。

2. 爸爸妈妈常打电话我。

3. 我们去超市下午四点半。

4. 在我的房间晚上六点举行生日晚会。

5. 今天是周末，他在食堂不吃饭。

6. 十二个朋友们参加我的生日晚会。

（七）根据实际情况回答问题 Answer the following questions according to the real situations

1. 今天几月几号？

2. 明天星期几？

3. 这个周末你去哪儿？

4. 你什么时候去？

5. 你和谁一起去？

6. 今天晚上你在哪儿吃饭？

（八）用下列偏旁写出至少三个汉字 Write out at least three characters with the following radicals

纟：＿＿＿＿＿＿＿＿＿＿＿＿＿＿＿ 八：＿＿＿＿＿＿＿＿＿＿＿＿＿＿＿

（九）描写汉字 Trace the following characters

第十二课 你的生日是什么时候

糕	米	粒	样	样	糕	糕	糕
啤	丶	丨	口	口'	口'	咀	畔	畔
	哩	啤
酒	丶	冫	氵	沪	沂	沔	洒	酒
	酒
打	一	十	才	扌	打
话	丶	讠	讠	讠	讠	话	话
祝	丶	丁	礻	礻	礻	礻	祝
快	丶	丶	忄	忄	快	快
送	丶	丷	丷	关	关	关	送	送
礼	丶	丁	礻	礻	礼
物	丿	𠂇	牛	牛	牜	物	物
唱	丨	口	口	叩	呾	唱	唱	唱
	唱	唱
歌	一	丁	可	可	可	哥	哥	哥
	哥	哥	歌	歌	歌
跳	丨	口	口	口	𧾷	𧾷	趴	趴
	趴	跳	跳	跳

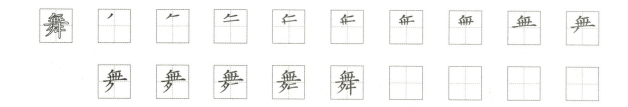

文化小贴士 Proverb

Shīfu lǐng jìn mén, xiūxíng zài gèrén.
师父领进门，修行在个人。

One can be an amateur with the help of the teacher,
but can't be a master without his own hard working.

第十三课
你最近学习怎么样

Lesson 13

How are you getting on with your study

这一课你将学到

语法项目 Grammar

1. 主谓谓语句
   我身体很好。　　　他工作很忙。

2. 疑问句（8）：用疑问代词"多"提问
   你今年多大？

3. 疑问句（9）：……怎么样？
   你最近学习怎么样？

重点词语 Key Words

1. 代词"有的"
   有的同学自己在宿舍做饭。

2. "二"和"两"
   十二　第二　二月　两位老师　两千　两万　两斤

3. 代词"每"
   我每天上午上课。

功能项目 Activities
询问、描述、写信

一 生词 New Words

1.	最近	n.	zuìjìn	recent time
2.	怎么样	pron.	zěnmeyàng	how about, what about
3.	多	pron.	duō	used in an interrogative sentence to ask about the number or degree
4.	比较	adv.	bǐjiào	relatively
5.	饭菜	n.	fàncài	meal, dish
6.	不错	adj.	búcuò	not bad, pretty good
7.	别的	pron.	biéde	else, other
8.	有的	pron.	yǒude	some
9.	自己	pron.	zìjǐ	oneself
10.	生活	n./v.	shēnghuó	life; live
11.	她们	pron.	tāmen	(female) they, them
12.	关心	v.	guānxīn	care, concern
13.	每	pron.	měi	every, each
14.	从	prep.	cóng	from, since, through
15.	但是	conj.	dànshì	but, yet, however
16.	有点儿	adv.	yǒudiǎnr	a little, a bit
17.	累	adj.	lèi	tired, weary, fatigued
18.	互相	adv.	hùxiāng	mutually, each other
19.	帮助	v.	bāngzhù	to help
20.	关系	n.	guānxi	relation, relationship
21.	非常	adv.	fēicháng	very, highly, extremely
22.	健康	adj.	jiànkāng	healthy
23.	儿子	n.	érzi	son

专名 Proper Noun

安德	Āndé	name of a male

第十三课　你最近学习怎么样

本课新字 New Characters

最	近	怎	样	菜	错	自
己	活	心	每	从	但	累
互	相	关	系	非	常	健

二　课文 Texts

（一）你最近学习怎么样

Lǎoshī：　Āndé, nǐ jīnnián duō dà?
老师：　安德，你今年多大？

Āndé：　Wǒ jīnnián shíjiǔ suì.
安德：　我今年十九岁。

Lǎoshī：　Nǐ èrlínglíngyī nián chūshēng de ba?
老师：　你二零零一年出生的吧？

Āndé：　Duì.
安德：　对。

Lǎoshī：　Nǐ zuìjìn shēntǐ hǎo ma?
老师：　你最近身体好吗？

Āndé：　Hěn hǎo, xièxie.
安德：　很好，谢谢。

Lǎoshī：　Xuéxí zěnmeyàng?
老师：　学习怎么样？

Āndé：　Bǐjiào máng.
安德：　比较忙。

Lǎoshī：　Shítáng de fàncài zěnmeyàng?
老师：　食堂的饭菜怎么样？

安德: 不错,我常常在食堂吃饭。

老师: 别的同学也在食堂吃吗?

安德: 有的同学在食堂吃,有的同学自己在宿舍做。

(二) 我现在生活很好

爸爸妈妈:

你们好!你们身体好吗?

我现在生活很好。我的学校很漂亮,宿舍和食堂也不错。我们有两位汉语老师,她们很关心我们,常常帮助我们。我每天上午上课,上午有五节课,从八点到十一点五十。下午有的时候也上课。星期六、星期天休息。汉语比较难,但是很有意思。我每天学习都很努力。

我身体很好,学习比较忙,有的时候有点儿累。食堂的饭菜很不错,我每天都在食堂吃饭。我的同学都很好,我们互相学习,互相帮助,关系非常好。

祝你们身体健康!

你们的儿子:安德

九月三十日

三 注 释 Notes

（一）你二零零一年出生的吧？ You were born in 2001, weren't you？

"吧"用于疑问句,表示委婉的询问,带有揣测语气,期待对方证实自己的揣测。如:

The word "吧" is used in an interrogative sentence, implying euphemistic inquiry, with the mode of guess and expecting an affirmative reply. For example:

(1) 你是中国人吧？

(2) 你们的老师都很好吧？

（二）从八点到十一点五十　From 8:00 to 11:50

"从"表示时间或空间的起点，"到"表示相应的终点。如：

The word "从" (from) means the start point of time or place, "到" (to) refers to the corresponding end. For example:

(1) 我从星期一到星期五都有课。

(2) 从我家到学校有点儿远。

四　汉字知识　About Chinese Characters

（一）怎样写好汉字（7）：稳中有变
Write characters beautifully (7) : Changes in alikeness

前面几课介绍的是写好汉字的基本规则。要想真正把汉字写得美观，还要在基本规则的基础上有所变化。许多汉字往往有几个相同的笔画，或由相同的部分组成，这些字如果只按照基本来写，相同的笔画、相同的部分都写得一样，字就显得非常呆板，没有生气。如：

Basic rules are introduced in the previous lessons to write characters well. In order to write characters beautifully, changes are necessary in the basic rules. It is often the case that a character consists of some strokes alike or of some parts alike. If these characters are written only according to the basic rules, and the same strokes or same elements are written the same, the character would look stiff, with no vitality. For example:

所以，在书写汉字时要注意"稳中有变"，即在遵守基本规则的基础上，使一些笔画有所变化。其基本方法是：

Therefore, in writing a Chinese character, keep the principle of "稳中有变" (changes in alikeness) in mind, which means to make some changes to the same strokes in a character. The following are some of the basic methods:

一笔正，另一笔斜　straight and slant：天　青

一笔短，另一笔长　long and short：童　毛

一笔直，另一笔曲　straight and bent：反　庐

一笔收，另一笔放　control and release：　逢　双

本教材所教汉字书写的基本要素，只是学习书写的最基本的方法。不过，只要能够较熟练地掌握，写出来的汉字就不会很难看。

The basic rules in writing characters taught in this book are the most basic methods of learning to write. If you can master these methods skillfully, you can write good Chinese characters.

（二）偏旁：广、心　　Radicals: "广" and "心"

1.
广字旁
guǎngzìpáng

用在字的外部，广字旁的字一般与房屋或场所有关。如："床、店"。
Radical "广" is used as the outside component of a character, implying a house or a place. For example: "床，店".

2.
心字底
xīnzìdǐ

用在字的最下面。心字底的字一般与人的心理活动有关。如："意、思"。
It is used at the bottom of a character, which implies the meaning of one's mental activities. For example: "意，思".

五　语法 Grammar

（一）主谓谓语句　The sentence with a subject-predicate phrase as the predicate

　　用主谓短语做谓语的句子叫主谓谓语句。顾名思义，主谓谓语句的最大特点是：它的谓语部分是由一个小的主语和谓语组成的主谓短语。如：

It refers that the predicate of a sentence is a subject-predicate phrase. According to the title, the distinguished characteristic is that the predicate consists of a sub-subject and a sub-predicate. For example：

妈妈身体很好。

　　例句中小主语"身体"和谓语"很好"构成主谓短语，做整个句子主语"妈妈"的谓语。

In this sentence, "身体", the sub-subject and "很好", the sub-predicate form the predicate of "妈妈", which is the subject of the sentence.

主谓谓语句中，句子主语和小主语的关系主要有两种：一种为小主语是大主语的一部分，如"我头疼"，小主语"头"是大主语"我（的身体）"的一个组成部分；另一种为小主语是大主语某一方面的情况，如"丁荣学习很努力"，大主语"丁荣"在小主语"学习"方面"很努力"。

In the sentence with a subject-predicate phrase as the predicate, there are two kinds of relationships between the main subject and the sub-subject. One is that the sub-subject is a part of the main subject. For example, in the sentence "我头疼", "头" is a part of "我（my body）". The other is that the sub-subject describes a certain aspect of the main subject. For example, in the sentence "丁荣学习很努力", "丁荣", the main subject works hard in his study (sub-subject).

大主语（S）	谓语（P）	
	小主语（S'）	小谓语（P'）
妈妈	身体	很好
丁荣	学习	很努力

大主语和小主语中间可以加上"的"，意思基本不变，但句子就变成了一般的主谓句。主谓谓语句在口语中用得较多，它常用来对人或事物从某一方面进行说明描写或评议判断。

The word "的" can be added between the main subject and the sub-subject, and the meaning remains the same. However, the sentence becomes an ordinary S-P sentence. The sentence with a subject-predicate phrase as the predicate is widely used in oral Chinese. It is often used to describe one aspect of somebody or something or to make comments.

主谓谓语句的否定形式是在小谓语处进行否定，而不是对整个句子的谓语进行否定。如：

The negative form is made by putting the negative verb before the sub-predicate, not the predicate of the whole sentence. For example:

妈妈身体很好。否定形式为： 妈妈身体不好。（√）

*妈妈不身体好。（×）

（二）疑问句（8）：用疑问代词"多"提问
Interrogative sentences (8) : Questions with "多"

疑问代词"多"用在疑问句中询问数量或程度。如：
"多" is an interrogative pronoun, inquiring the quantity or degree in an interrogative sentence. For example:

(1) 你今年多大？

(2) 从你的宿舍到图书馆有多远？

"多"后边的形容词常常是"大""高""长""远"等，注意不能用它们的反义词。如："* 多小""* 多矮""* 多短""* 多近"等。
Most of the adjectives after "多" are "大 , 高 , 长" and "远", but not their antonyms, such as: "* 多小 , * 多矮 , * 多短 , * 多近", etc.

"多"的前边可以用"有"。如：
The word "有" can be added before "多". For example:

(1) 从你家到学校（有）多远？

(2) 那座黄色的大楼（有）多高？

（三）疑问句（9）：……怎么样？
Interrogative sentences (9) : Questions with "怎么样"

疑问代词"怎么样"可以构成特指疑问句，用于询问状况。"怎么样"用于句尾，做谓语或宾语。如：
Special interrogatives can be formed by "怎么样", which asks a question. It is used as a predicate or object at the end of an interrogative. For example:

(1) 你身体怎么样？

(2) 电影怎么样？

"怎么样"也可以用在陈述句后，单独成句，有商量的意味。如：
The word "怎么样" can also be used after a declarative sentence independently, implying consultation. For example:

(1) 我们一起去，怎么样？

(2) 我们在宿舍举行生日晚会，怎么样？

六 重点词语 Key Words

（一）代词"有的" Pronoun "有的"

代词"有的"表示人或事物中的一部分。如：
The pronoun "有的" means one part of people or things. For example:

(1) 我们班有的同学发音不太好。

(2) 有的书很难，有的书不难。

（二）"二"和"两" 二 (two) and 两 (double, twin)

"二"和"两"都是"2"的意思，但用法不同。
Both of them mean two, but in different ways.

二 two：

(1) 数数时读：Read in counting：

一、二、三……十二……一百三十二……

(2) 称数序数时读：Read as an ordinal number：

第二 二月 二楼 二班

(3) 用在"十/百"之前时读：Read before "十/百"：

二十 二百

(4) 用在度量衡量词"两"之前时读：
Read before the measure word "两"：

二两

另外，房间号码、电话号码、车牌号码中的"2"都读作"二"。
Besides, it is read "二" in room numbers, telephone numbers and vehicle plate numbers.

两 two：

(1) 用在量词前：Used before a measure word：

两个　两位　两本

(2) 用在"千/万"之前：Used before "千/万"：

两千　两万

(3) 用在度量衡量词之前：Used before a measure word：

两斤 (two *jins*)　两千米 (two kilometers)　两米 (two meters)

（三）代词"每" Pronoun "每"

代词"每"指全体中的任何个体，代表全体。"每"常用在数量词的前面，数词是"一"的时候，"一"常常省略。如：
The pronoun "每" refers to any single one of the whole, so it represents the whole. It is usually used before a number. When the number is "一" (one), it is usually omitted. For example:

(1) 每（一）件衣服都很漂亮。

(2) 我们班每个同学学习都很努力。

"每"的后面是表示年、月、日等时间词语时，用法不太一样。如：
When "每" is followed by time words, it is used differently. For example:

每年　每（个）月　每（个）星期　每天

不可以说：
The following expressions are wrong:

＊每个年　＊每个天

七　练习　Exercises

（一）朗读下面的短语　Read the following phrases

多大	多远	有点儿贵	有点儿难
有的人	有的国家	有的教室	有的房间
自己学习	自己生活	关心同学	关心别人
每天	每年	每（个）月	每（个）星期
每位老师	每个同学	每门课	每件衣服
两个	两天	两岁	两块钱
两千二百一十二	二年级	二月二号	二楼二零二房间
从家到学校	从宿舍到教室	从两点到六点	从早上到晚上

（二）替换练习　Substitutions

1. A：你今年多大?
   B：我今年十九岁。

你爸爸	五十一
你姐姐	二十七
王老师	三十三
丁荣	二十

2. A：食堂的饭菜怎么样?
   B：不错。

你的学校	很好
那件衣服	很漂亮
汉语	有点儿难
今天的天气	不太好

3. A：你们身体好吗?
   B：很好。

爸爸	工作	忙
安德	学习	努力
你们学校	老师	好
你们国家	水果	贵

4．有的 留学生 是 美国人。

书	是	丁荣的
学生	回	宿舍
水果	很	便宜
外国人	喜欢	中国菜

（三）选词填空　Choose and fill in the blanks

吧　　自己　　有点儿　　关心　　从……到……

1．今天他 _____ 不高兴。

2．老师很 _____ 我们的学习。

3．我在学校的时候，常常 _____ 做饭。

4．你是一年级三班的学生 _____ ？

5．_____ 宿舍 _____ 食堂不太远。

每　　生活　　健康　　帮助　　最近

1．你 _____ 身体怎么样？

2．我的朋友常常 _____ 我学习汉语。

3．我在中国的 _____ 很有意思。

4．祝你身体 _____ 。

5．上课的时候，_____ 个人都说汉语。

（四）用"二"和"两"填空　Fill in the blanks with "二" and "两"

1．我们学校有 _____ 万多个学生。

2．我是一年级 _____ 班的学生。

3．我今年 _____ 月来中国。

4．星期五下午有 _____ 节课。

5．这 _____ 件衣服是你买的吗？

6．我们班有 _____ 十 _____ 个留学生。

（五）完成对话　Complete the following dialogues

1. A：_____？
   B：我学习汉语。

2. A：_____？
   B：我买三斤苹果。

3. A：_____？
   B：我的爸爸是医生。

4. A：_____？
   B：丁荣在北京大学学习。

5. A：_____？
   B：比较忙。

6. A：_____？
   B：不太好。

（六）连词成句　Make sentences with the given words

1. 他　　很　　学习　　努力
   _____

2. 最近　　我　　不太　　身体　　好
   _____

3. 我　　和　　同屋　　关系　　非常　　的　　好
   _____

4. 从……到……　工作　　妈妈　　星期一　　星期五　　都
   _____

5. 在食堂　　别的　　吃饭　　同学　　也
   _____

6. 儿子　　的　　多大　　王老师　　今年
   _____

7. 每天 图书馆 我 去 都

_____

8. 的 我们班 同学 关心 互相

_____

（七）根据提示词语，看图写句子　Make sentences according to the given words and pictures

累　　　　　关心　　　　　有的　　　　　饭菜

（八）用下列偏旁写出至少三个汉字　Write out at least three characters with the following radicals

广：_____　　　　心：_____

（九）描写汉字　Trace the following characters

最

近

怎

样

菜	一	十	艹	艹	艹	芊	苙	荬	菜
	菜	菜							
错	丿	𠂉	𠂉	钅	钅	钅	钭	错	错
	错	错	错						
关	丶	丷	丷	关	关				
心	丶	心	心	心					
每	丿	𠂉	𠂉	每	每	每	每		
从	丿	人	从	从					
累	丶	冂	田	田	甲	里	畀	累	
	累	累							
互	一	丁	互	互					
相	一	十	才	木	朾	机	机	相	相
自	丿	丨	自	自	自	自			
己	乛	𠃌	己						
活	丶	氵	氵	汗	汗	活	活	活	
帮	一	二	三	丰	邦	邦	帮	帮	
助	丨	冂	日	日	且	助	助		
系	一	𠃋	幺	幺	爫	系	系		

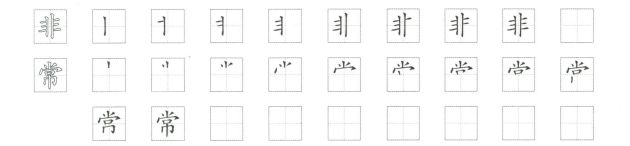

文化小贴士 Proverb

Zǎo shuì zǎo qǐ shēntǐ hǎo.
早睡早起身体好。

Early to bed and early to rise makes a man healthy.

第十四课
我们坐地铁去吧

14 Lesson
Let's go by metro

这一课你将学到

语法项目　Grammar

1. 动作的进行：正、在、正在、……呢
   我 正 / 在 / 正在 看电视呢。

2. 连动句
   我们一起去公园玩儿吧。　　我们坐地铁去。

3. 疑问句（10）：……，好吗？
   我们一起去公园玩儿，好吗？

4. 疑问句（11）：……怎么……？
   我们怎么去？

重点词语　Key Words

1. 或者
   骑自行车，坐公共汽车或者坐地铁都可以。

2. 还
   公园里有一个很大的湖，还有很多树和花儿。

3. 跟
   我们用汉语跟中国人聊天儿。

功能项目　Activities
打电话、相约

一 生词 New Words

1.	坐	v.	zuò	take, travel by
2.	地铁	n.	dìtiě	metro, subway
3.	喂	interj.	wèi	hello, hey
4.	就	adv.	jiù	exactly
5.	正在	adv.	zhèngzài	in the process of, in the course of
	正	adv.	zhèng	in the process of, in the course of
	在	adv.	zài	in the process of, in the course of
6.	呢	particle	ne	used at the end of interrogative sentence to indicate certain kind of mood
7.	电视	n.	diànshì	television, TV
8.	空儿	n.	kòngr	free time
9.	骑	v.	qí	ride (an animal or bicycle)
10.	自行车	n.	zìxíngchē	bicycle, bike
11.	或者	conj.	huòzhě	or
12.	汽车	n.	qìchē	car
	公共汽车	n.	gōnggòng qìchē	bus
	出租车	n.	chūzūchē	taxi
13.	可以	adj.	kěyǐ	ok
14.	里	n.	lǐ	inside, interior
15.	湖	n.	hú	lake
16.	还	adv.	hái	also, too
17.	树	n.	shù	tree
18.	花儿	n.	huār	flower

19.	风景	n.	fēngjǐng	scenery, landscape, sights
20.	空气	n.	kōngqì	air, atmosphere
21.	散步		sàn bù	take a walk, go for a walk
22.	可爱	adj.	kě'ài	lovable, lovely
23.	孩子	n.	háizi	child, kid
24.	草地	n.	cǎodì	lawn, meadow
25.	用	v.	yòng	use
26.	跟	prep.	gēn	with, together
27.	聊天儿		liáo tiānr	chat
28.	午饭	n.	wǔfàn	midday meal, lunch

本课新字 New Characters

坐	铁	喂	正	视	空	骑	车
或	者	汽	租	里	树	花	风
景	散	步	爱	孩	草	用	聊

二 课文 Texts

（一）我们坐地铁去吧

Lǐ Míng'ài： Wèi, nǐ hǎo, qǐngwèn Dīng Róng zài ma?
李明爱：喂，你好，请问 丁荣 在吗？

Dīng Róng： Wǒ jiù shì, nǐ shì nǎ wèi?
丁 荣：我就是，你是哪位？

李明爱：我是李明爱，你在做什么呢？

丁荣：李明爱，你好。我正看电视呢，你有事儿吗？

李明爱：你明天有没有空儿？我们一起去公园玩儿，好吗？

丁荣：好，我们怎么去？

李明爱：骑自行车、坐公共汽车或者坐地铁都可以。

丁荣：我没有自行车，我们坐地铁去吧。

李明爱：好，我们明天上午九点在一楼见，怎么样？

丁荣：好，明天见。

李明爱：明天见。

（二）有的人正在散步

今天我和李明爱坐地铁去公园玩儿。公园里有一个很大的湖，还有很多树和花儿，风景很漂亮，空气也非常好。公园里人很多，有的正在散步，有的正在锻炼身体。还有很多可爱的孩子，他们在草地上玩儿，非常高

xìng. Wǒ hé Lǐ Míng'ài zài gōngyuán li sàn bù, yòng Hànyǔ gēn Zhōngguórén liáo tiānr,
兴。我和李明爱在 公园 里散步,用汉语 跟 中国人 聊天儿,
hěn yǒu yìsi. Zhōngwǔ wǒmen zài yí ge xiǎo fànguǎnr chī wǔfàn, wǔfàn yǐhòu zuò
很有意思。中午 我们在一个 小 饭馆儿 吃午饭, 午饭以后 坐
chūzūchē huí sùshè. Jīntiān wǒmen hěn gāoxìng.
出租车 回宿舍。今天 我们 很 高兴。

三 注释 Notes

（一）我就是。 It's me exactly.

"就"表示强调、肯定的语气,意思是"是这个,不是别的"。如:

The word "就" implies the mood of emphasis and affirmation. It means: It is this one, not others. For example:

(1) 这位老师就是我们的汉语老师。

(2) 图书馆就在办公楼的前边。

（二）公园里有一个很大的湖。 There is a very large lake in the park.

此处"有"表示存在，说明某处所存在着某人或某事物。
The word "有" in this sentence means "exist", implies that there is somebody or something in somewhere.

（三）交通工具 Vehicles

这一课我们学习了一些交通工具，还有一些常用的交通工具，如下图所示：
We have learnt some vehicles in this lesson. There are also some frequently used vehicles showed in the following pictures:

摩托车	mótuōchē	motorcycle
长途客车	chángtú kèchē	coach
飞机	fēijī	plane, airplane
船	chuán	ship
火车	huǒchē	train
高铁	gāotiě	high-speed train

四 》 汉字知识 About Chinese Characters

（一）偏旁：王、木 Radicals: "王" and "木"

1. 王字旁 wángzìpáng

用在字的左边，"王"本义为玉石，因此王字旁的字多与玉石有关。如："班、玩"。
It is used as the left component of a character. The original meaning of "王" is jade, so characters with radical "王" has the meaning of jade. For example: "班，玩".

2. 木字旁 mùzìpáng

用在字的左边，木字旁源于"木"字，木字旁的字一般与木本植物有关。如："树、样"。
It is used as the left component of a character, the meaning is related to the woody plants. For example: "树，样".

189

五　语　法　Grammar

（一）动作的进行　Processing of an action

动词的前面加上副词"正""在""正在"或在句尾加"呢",表示动作的进行。如：
The adverbs "正" "在" and "正在" added prior to the verbs, or "呢" at the end of a sentence, indicate that an action is in progress. For example:

(1) 妈妈正在做饭。

(2) 小明在看电视。

(3) A：你做什么呢？

　　B：我看书呢。

"正""在""正在"也可以与"呢"同时使用,如：
"正" "在" or "正在" can also be used together with "呢". For example:

(4) 我正上课呢。

(5) 爸爸在打电话呢。

(6) 我到宿舍的时候，他们正在聊天儿呢。

"正（在）"强调动作正在进行,具有时间"点"的特点；而"在"强调动作的持续,具有时间"段"的特点。如例（4）、例（6）强调在说话的那个时间点进行的动作是"上课""聊天儿"；例（5）强调"打电话"这个动作的进行和持续。
The word "正（在）" emphasizes that the action is taking place right now, focusing on a certain time point. While "在" emphasizes the continuance of an action, focusing on a certain period of time. In the above examples, No. 4 and No.6 focus on that at the time point of speaking, "上课" (having a class) and "聊天儿"(chatting) are taking place. No.5 focuses on the processing and continuance of "打电话" (making a phone call).

否定时可以直接用"没（有）"作简单回答。如：
"没（有）" can be used as a negative reply. For example:

(7) A：你在休息吗？

　　B：没有，我打扫房间呢。

也可以把"没（有）"放在动词短语前，否定动作行为。如：
"没（有）" can also be used before the verbal construction to give a negative answer. For example:

(8) A：你正在看电视吗？

B：我没在看电视，我正在看书。

（二）连动句 Sentences with verbal constructions in series

连动句的谓语由两个或两个以上的动词短语构成，它们之间没有停顿，也不使用关联词语。如：

The predicate of a sentence with verbal construction in series consists of two or more verb constructions, among which there is no stop or conjuction. For example:

(1) 我们一起去公园玩儿。

(2) 我们坐地铁去。

连动句根据谓语中两个动词短语之间的意义关系，可以分为以下两种：
There are two kinds of sentences according to the relationship between the two verbs meaning:

1. 后一个动词短语表示的动作行为是前一个动词短语表示的动作行为的目的。如：
The action of the later verb indicates the purpose of the former. For example:

(1) 我来中国学习汉语。

(2) 我去图书馆借书。

2. 一个动词短语表示后一个动词短语所表示的动作的方式、手段、工具等。如：
The former V-O phrase implies the means, manner or tools of the later. For example:

(1) 妈妈骑自行车上班。

(2) 我用电脑写信。

（三）疑问句（10）：用"……，好吗"提问
Interrogative sentences (10): Ask questions with "……，好吗"

"……，好吗"表示提出建议，征求对方意见。有商量、请求的意思，也可以用"好不好"。如：

This kind of questions is a suggestion to ask the opinion of the listener. "好不好" can be used to mean requiring or consulting. For example:

(1) 我们一起去，好吗（好不好）？

(2) 我们在食堂吃饭，好吗（好不好）？

（四）疑问句（11）：用"怎么"提问
Interrogative sentences (11): Ask questions with "怎么"

"怎么"放在动词的前面，询问动作的方式、手段、工具等。如：

"怎么" is used before a verb, inquiring the methods, manner or tools of an action. For example:

(1) A：我们怎么去？

　　B：坐公共汽车去吧。

(2) A：这个汉字怎么读？

　　B：读"yáng"。

六　重点词语 Key Words

（一）"还是"和"或者"　"还是"and"或者"

"还是"和"或者"都表示选择的意思。二者的区别主要是"还是"用在问句中，"或者"用在陈述句中。如：

Both "还是" and "或者" mean alternative. "还是" is mainly used in an interrogative sentence, while "或者" is usually used in a declarative sentence. For example:

(1) A：你要大的还是要小的？

　　B：我要大的。

(2) A：你吃苹果还是西瓜？
　　B：苹果或者西瓜都可以。

（二）副词"还"　Adverb "还"

"还"，副词。表示在某个范围外有所补充，用在动词前。如：
The word "还" is an adverb, meaning to add something else besides what is mentioned. It is used before a verb. For example:

(1) 我买了两斤苹果，还买了三斤香蕉。

(2) 我喜欢汉语，还喜欢中国文化。

（三）跟　Conjunction "跟"

"跟"，连词，跟指人的名词组合，表示共同、协同。"跟"连接的两个名词互换位置，句子意思不变。"跟"也可以和"一起"连用。如：
The word "跟" is a conjunction, by combining with personal nouns, it means "cooperating" "together". If the two nouns connected by "跟" reversed, the meaning of the sentences remains the same. "跟" can also be used together with "一起". For example:

(1) 我跟李明爱在公园散步。

(2) 我跟李明爱一起去公园。

"跟"还可以指示与动作有关的对方，这时是介词。"跟"前后的两个名词互换位置，句子意思有点儿不一样。如：
It can also indicate the other part concerned in the action, under this condition, "跟" is a preposition. If the two nouns connected by "跟" reversed, the meaning of the sentence is a little different. For example:

(1) 我们跟中国人聊天儿。　≠　中国人跟我们聊天儿。

(2) 我常常跟朋友联系。　≠　朋友常常跟我联系。

七 练习 Exercises

（一）朗读下面的短语 Read the following phrases

正在吃饭	正在休息	正睡觉呢	正打电话呢
有空儿	没空儿	跟朋友聊天儿	跟同学聊天儿
怎么说	怎么写	怎么唱	怎么跳（tiào, jump）
公园里	学校里	房间里	书包里
可爱的小孩儿	很可爱	还吃包子	还买苹果
骑车来学校	坐车回家	去公园散步	去超市买东西
用英语聊天儿	用法语聊天儿	用人民币买东西	用美元买东西

（二）替换练习 Substitutions

1. A：你做什么呢？
   B：我<u>看书</u>呢。

   看电视
   买东西
   吃午饭
   在公园散步
   给爸爸妈妈发微信

2. A：<u>他</u>正在做什么？
   B：<u>他正在学习汉语</u>。

爸爸	看手机
妈妈	做饭
他们	上课
那个人	跑步（pǎo bù, run）

3. A：我们一起<u>去公园</u> <u>玩儿</u>，好吗？
   B：好吧。

去外面	吃饭
回宿舍	休息
去教室	上课
做饭	吃

4. A：我们怎么去那儿？　　　　　坐公共汽车
　　B：骑自行车去吧。　　　　　　坐出租车
　　　　　　　　　　　　　　　　坐火车 (huǒchē, train)
　　　　　　　　　　　　　　　　坐飞机 (fēijī, plane)

5. 我有一个哥哥，还有一个妹妹。　买　　两支铅笔　　三个本子
　　　　　　　　　　　　　　　　吃　　一个苹果　　一个香蕉
　　　　　　　　　　　　　　　　学习　英语　　　　汉语

6. 我跟李明爱一起去公园。　　　　我　　他　　　　一起学习汉语
　　　　　　　　　　　　　　　　我们　中国人　　　聊天儿
　　　　　　　　　　　　　　　　安德　安达　　　　是好朋友

（三）选词填空　Choose and fill in the blanks

怎么　　怎么样

1. 你_____过生日？

2. 你的汉语_____？

3. 英语"taxi"，汉语_____说？

4. 你_____去上海？

5. 你看，这件衣服_____？

还是　　或者

1. 你是老师_____学生？

2. 今天去_____明天去都可以。

3. 王老师_____田老师都可以帮助你。

4. 你买苹果_____买香蕉？

5. 你怎么付，微信_____支付宝？

（四）改错 Correct the following sentences

1. 我和李明爱一起买本子去商店。

2. 王老师明天去上海坐飞机。

3. 下课以后我回宿舍还是去食堂。

4. 我在认识一个新朋友呢。

5. 张老师正在是我们班的汉语老师。

6. 我不常聊天儿中国人。

7. 安德学习很努力，丁荣学习还很努力。

（五）用所给的词完成对话 Complete the following dialogues with the given words

1. A：你看什么呢？
   B：_____。（正）

2. A：_____？（怎么）
   B：我用 E-mail 给爸爸妈妈写信。

3. A：你吃什么？
   B：_____。（或者）

4. A：你周末怎么过？
   B：_____。（坐）

5. A：_____？（喂）
   B：我就是。

6. A：你自己去吗？
   B：_____。（跟）

（六）连词成句 Make sentences with the given words

1. 教　　老师　　唱歌　　我们　　正在

2. 常常　　星期六或者星期天　　玩儿　　去公园　　我们
   _____

3. 我　　在公园　　跟　　散步　　李明爱　　一起
   _____

4. 微信　　付　　用　　钱　　我们
   _____

5. 我　　周末　　在宿舍　　做饭　　吃
   _____

6. 跟　　聊天儿呢　　老师　　他　　正
   _____

（七）用下列偏旁写出至少三个汉字　Write out at least three characters with the following radicals

　　　王：_____　　　　木：_____

（八）根据提示词语，看图写句子　Make sentences according to the given words and pictures

　　地铁　　　　风景　　　　可爱　　　　聊天儿　　　　骑

（九）写作　Writing

从下面词语中至少选用3—5个，写你出去玩儿的一次经历，字数不少于80字。
Choose at least 3—5 words or phrases to describe one of your sightseeings, no less than 80 characters.

骑　　　　坐　　　　玩儿　　　　散步　　　　聊天儿　　　　锻炼
有的……，有的……　　　　有意思　　　　可爱　　　　正在
天气　　　　公园　　　　风景　　　　空气　　　　树　　　　花儿

（十）描写汉字　Trace the following characters

喂	丨	口	口	叩	叩	呵	呷	呷	喂
	喂	喂	喂						
正	一	丁	下	止	正				
视	丶	⼀	㇇	礻	衤	衤	视	视	
空	丶	丷	宀	穴	穴	空	空	空	
骑	㇇	马	马	马	驭	驭	骈	骑	骑
	骑	骑							
车	一	𠂇	左	车					
铁	丿	㇇	㇇	钅	钅	钅	钅	铁	
	铁								
或	一	丆	冂	戸	戸	或	或	或	
者	一	十	土	耂	耂	者	者	者	
坐	丿	人	从	从	坐	坐	坐		
汽	丶	氵	氵	汽	汽	汽	汽		
里	丨	口	曰	日	甲	甲	里		

文化小贴士 Proverb

Qiān lǐ zhī xíng, Shǐ yú zú xià.
千里之行，始于足下。

A long trip starts from the first step.

第十五课
复习（三）

Lesson 15 Review (III)

一 生词 New Words

1.	去年	n.	qùnián	last year
2.	大学	n.	dàxué	university
3.	毕业		bì yè	graduate
4.	当	v.	dāng	act as, work as, serve as, be
5.	翻译	n./v.	fānyì	translator, interpreter; translate
6.	陪	v.	péi	accompany
7.	城市	n.	chéngshì	city
8.	出去	v	chūqù	go out
9.	小学	n.	xiǎoxué	primary school
10.	个子	n.	gèzi	height
11.	高	adj.	gāo	tall, high
12.	下	n.	xià	next
13.	打算	v./n.	dǎsuàn	plan
14.	香水	n.	xiāngshuǐ	perfume

一 本课新字 New Characters

毕 业 当 翻 译 陪
城 市 出 高 算 香

二 课文 Text

我的哥哥

Wǒ gēge jīnnián èrshísì suì. Tā qùnián dàxué bì yè, zài yì jiā gōngsī
我哥哥今年二十四岁。他去年大学毕业,在一家公司
dāng fānyì. Gēge gōngzuò hěn máng, měi tiān wǎnshang hěn wǎn huí jiā, yǒude
当翻译。哥哥工作很忙,每天晚上很晚回家,有的
shíhou zhōumò yě shàng bān, hái chángcháng péi gōngsī jīnglǐ qù biéde chéngshì.
时候周末也上班,还常常陪公司经理去别的城市。
Gēge yǒu hěn duō péngyou, yǒu Zhōngguó de, yǒu wàiguó de, měi ge rén dōu hěn
哥哥有很多朋友,有中国的,有外国的,每个人都很
xǐhuan tā. Tā chángcháng gēn péngyoumen chūqù chī fàn、liáo tiānr, yìqǐ wánr.
喜欢他。他常常跟朋友们出去吃饭、聊天儿,一起玩儿。
Gēge yǒu yí ge nǚ péngyou, shì xiǎoxué Yīngyǔ lǎoshī. Tā gèzi hěn gāo, hěn
哥哥有一个女朋友,是小学英语老师。她个子很高,很

送香水她会喜欢吗?

你的女朋友肯定很喜欢。

piàoliang. Xià xīngqī'èr shì tā de shēngrì, gēge dǎsuàn sòng tā yì píng Fǎguó
漂亮。下星期二是她的生日，哥哥打算送她一瓶法国
xiāngshuǐ. Zhè zhǒng xiāngshuǐ yǒudiǎnr guì, yì píng jiǔ bǎi bāshí kuài qián, dànshì
香水。这种香水有点儿贵，一瓶九百八十块钱，但是
gēge de nǚ péngyou yídìng hěn xǐhuan.
哥哥的女朋友一定很喜欢。

三 练习 Exercises

（一）根据课文内容判断正误 Judge the following sentences true or false according to the text

1. 哥哥二十四岁大学毕业。　　　　　　　（　）
2. 哥哥在公司工作。　　　　　　　　　　（　）
3. 哥哥晚上常常不回家。　　　　　　　　（　）
4. 哥哥在别的城市工作。　　　　　　　　（　）
5. 哥哥有很多外国朋友。　　　　　　　　（　）
6. 哥哥的女朋友是大学英语老师。　　　　（　）
7. 这个星期二是哥哥女朋友的生日。　　　（　）
8. 哥哥打算送女朋友一件衣服。　　　　　（　）

（二）选词填空 Choose and fill in the blanks

当　　城市　　打算　　高　　陪

1. 下午，我_____同屋去书店买书。

2. 大学毕业以后，我想_____医生。

3. 北京是中国的一个大_____。

4. 我_____去中国学习汉语。

5. 我的姐姐个子不太_____。

翻译　　经理　　下　　小学　　有的

1. _____ 苹果是红色的，_____ 苹果是绿色的。

2. 你给我 _____ 一下这个句子（jùzi, sentence），好吗？

3. _____ 个月 15 号是我爸爸的生日。

4. 小明的爸爸是一家公司的 _____。

5. 我妈妈是 _____ 老师。

（三）完成对话　　Complete the following dialogues

1. A：你爸爸妈妈好吗？

   B：_____。

2. A：_____？

   B：中国人用筷子 (kuàizi, chopsticks) 吃饭。

3. A：你去办公室做什么？

   B：_____。

4. A：_____？

   B：我哥哥坐飞机去美国。

5. A：喂，你好，请问王老师在吗？

   B：_____。

6. A：你们学校的留学生宿舍怎么样？

   B：_____。

7. A：_____？

   B：我正在上网看电影。

8. A：_____？

   B：我喝茶或者咖啡都可以。

9. A：你跟我一起学习汉语，好吗？

   B：_____。

10．A：哪辆 (liàng, measure word for vehicle) 自行车是你的？

　　B：_____。

（四）连词成句　Make sentences with the given words

1．我们　一点儿　买　吧　吃的

_____

2．我　做饭　妈妈　非常　好吃

_____

3．我　今天　努力　从……开始　学习

_____

4．我　同屋　帮　买早饭　经常

_____

5．骑　自行车　姐姐　看风景　公园　去

_____

6．你　中国电影　外国电影　喜欢看　还是

_____

7．他　女朋友　在　打　电话　呢　给

_____

8．星期六　在　举行　晚会　我的　生日　房间

_____

（五）改错　Correct the following sentences

1．我有二个中国朋友。

2．怎么样你的身体最近？

3．我们班有的同学都很努力。

4．我今天一点儿累。

5．波伟买词典去书店。

6. 我们学校每个年都有新的留学生。

7. 你喝茶或者咖啡？

8. 这个小孩儿今年多大岁？

（六）阅读　Reading comprehension

　　今天上课的时候，老师问同学们在中国的生活怎么样。我说我在中国生活很好，我喜欢我的学校，喜欢我的老师和同学，我也喜欢学习汉语。汉语虽然很难，但是很有意思。我每天锻炼身体，身体也很好。

　　我们班的每个学生都说了自己的生活。有的说中国的城市很漂亮，在中国生活很舒服；有的说自己很忙，学习很努力，生活很充实（chōngshí, fulfilling）。波伟说他每天起床很难，他喜欢睡觉，别的都很好。丁荣说她不太喜欢吃食堂的饭菜，所以每天自己在宿舍做饭，有点儿麻烦（máfan, trouble some）。李明爱说她在中国很高兴，中国的风景很漂亮，没有课的时候，她常常骑自行车出去看看风景，她想以后去中国别的城市旅行（lǚxíng, travel）。

根据短文判断正误　Judge the following statements true or false according to the passage

1. 我在中国生活很舒服。　　　　　　　　　　　　（　　）
2. 我们班的同学学习都很努力，也都很忙。　　　　（　　）
3. 波伟每天起床很晚。　　　　　　　　　　　　　（　　）
4. 丁荣每天自己在宿舍做饭。　　　　　　　　　　（　　）
5. 李明爱在中国很高兴，她常出去买东西。　　　　（　　）
6. 我们班有的同学很喜欢中国的城市和风景。　　　（　　）

（七）根据提示词语，看图写句子　Make sentences according to the given words and pictures

正在

打算

城市

翻译

陪

（八）写作　Writing

从下面的词语中至少选用3—5个，写写你在中国的生活。
Choose at least 3—5 words or phrases from the following to describe your life in China.

| 从……到…… | 但是 | 漂亮 | 喜欢 | 练习 | 聊天儿 | 买 |
| 学习 | 起床 | 上课 | 休息 | 睡觉 | 玩儿 | |

（九）根据偏旁给下列汉字归类，并写出偏旁　Sort the following characters according to their radicals and write out the radicals of each group

操　场　花　红　漂　现　蕉　怎　样　忙　意　扰
节　哪　派　庭　活　找　蓝　汽　床　绿　树　绍
机　打　思　叫　给　班　喝　喂　楼　息　草　级
玩　菜　康　没　球　苹　汉　经　呢　理　店

例　口：哪　叫　喝　喂　呢

____ : _____　　　____ : _____

____ : _____　　　____ : _____

____ : _____　　　____ : _____

____ : _____　　　____ : _____

____ : _____　　　____ : _____

____ : _____　　　____ : _____

（十）描写汉字　Trace the following characters

毕　｜　上　比　比　比　毕

第十五课 复习（三）

🌱 文化小贴士 Proverb

Zài jiā kào fùmǔ, chū mén kào péngyou.
在家靠父母，出门靠朋友。

Parents can be relied at home while friends can be relied outward.

207

第十六课
晚上听听音乐，看看电视

Lesson 16
Listening to the music or watching TV in the evening

这一课你将学到

语法项目　Grammar

1. 动词重叠
   晚上听听音乐，看看电视。

2. "呢"和省略问句
   我有时候去逛逛商场，你呢？

3. 号码的读法
   318房间

4. 时刻表达法：点（钟）、分、刻、半
   七点一刻

重点词语　Key Words
副词"大概"
　　大概九点钟开始学习。

功能项目　Activities
日常生活、时间安排

第十六课 晚上听听音乐，看看电视

一、生词 New Words

1.	听	v.	tīng	listen, hear
2.	音乐	n.	yīnyuè	music
3.	复习	v.	fùxí	review
4.	预习	v.	yùxí	preview
5.	练习	n./v.	liànxí	exercise; practice
6.	电脑	n.	diànnǎo	computer
7.	上	v.	shàng	to be on (somewhere)
8.	网	n.	wǎng	internet
9.	新闻	n.	xīnwén	news
10.	发	v.	fā	deliver, send out
11.	朋友圈儿	n.	péngyouquānr	Moments
12.	平常	n.	píngcháng	ordinary time
13.	逛	v.	guàng	stroll
14.	商场	n.	shāngchǎng	shopping mall
15.	起床		qǐ chuáng	get up
16.	刻	m.	kè	quarter (of an hour)
17.	早饭	n.	zǎofàn	breakfast
18.	经常	adv.	jīngcháng	often
19.	差	v.	chà	short of
20.	大概	adv.	dàgài	probably
21.	操场	n.	cāochǎng	playground
22.	跑步		pǎo bù	run
23.	篮球	n.	lánqiú	basketball
24.	点钟	n.	diǎnzhōng	o'clock
25.	开始	v.	kāishǐ	begin, start

专名 Proper Noun

| 泰国 | Tàiguó | Thailand |

本课新字 New Characters

听	音	乐	复	预	练	脑	网
新	闻	发	逛	床	刻	经	常
差	概	操	场	跑	篮	钟	始

二 课 文 Texts

（一）晚上听听音乐，看看电视

Lǐ Míng'ài: Āndé, Nǐ xià kè yǐhòu chángcháng zuò shénme?
李明爱：安德，你下课以后常常做什么？

Āndé: Fùxí jiù kè, yùxí xīn kè, zuò liànxí, xiě Hànzì.
安德：复习旧课，预习新课，做练习，写汉字。

Lǐ Míng'ài: Nǐ bù xuéxí de shíhou zuò shénme?
李明爱：你不学习的时候做什么？

Āndé: Wánr diànnǎo, shàng wǎng kàn xīnwén, yǒushíhou kàn wēixìn.
安德：玩儿电脑，上网看新闻，有时候看微信。

Lǐ Míng'ài: Nǐ hǎoxiàng hěn shǎo fā péngyouquānr.
李明爱：你好像很少发朋友圈儿。

Āndé: Shìde, wǒ xǐhuan kàn, bù xǐhuan fā. Lǐ Míng'ài, nǐ píngcháng zuò shénme?
安德：是的，我喜欢看，不喜欢发。李明爱，你平常做什么？

李明爱：Xiàwǔ méiyǒu kè de shíhou, wǒ chángcháng qù cāochǎng dǎda qiú,
下午没有课的时候，我常常去操场打打球，
duànliàn duànliàn shēntǐ.
锻炼锻炼身体。

安德：Wǎnshang ne?
晚上呢？

李明爱：Wǎnshang tīngting yīnyuè, kànkan diànshì.
晚上听听音乐，看看电视。

安德：Nǐ zhōumò chūqu wánr ma?
你周末出去玩儿吗？

李明爱：Yǒushíhou qù gōngyuán wánrwanr, yǒushíhou qù guàngguang shāngchǎng.
有时候去公园玩儿玩儿，有时候去逛逛商场。
Nǐ ne?
你呢？

安德：Wǒ zhōumò dōu zài fángjiān shuì jiào.
我周末都在房间睡觉。

李明爱：Nǐ jǐ diǎn qǐ chuáng ne?
你几点起床呢？

安德：Shíyī diǎn ba.
十一点吧。

（二）我的同屋

Wǒ zhù sùshèlóu sān yāo bā fángjiān. Wǒ yǒu yí ge tóngwū, tā shì Tàiguórén,
我住宿舍楼318房间。我有一个同屋，他是泰国人，
jiào Bōwěi. Tā měi tiān qī diǎn qǐ chuáng, qī diǎn yíkè qù shítáng chī zǎofàn, tā
叫波伟。他每天七点起床，七点一刻去食堂吃早饭，他

经常帮我买早饭。我们八点上课,每天他都差十分八点到教室。午饭以后,从一点到两点半,他睡午觉。大概三点,他开始复习汉语课。下午五点的时候,他去操场锻炼身体,有时候跑步,有时候打篮球。他七点吃晚饭,大概九点钟开始学习,十一点半睡觉。波伟学习很好,人也很好,我们关系很好。

三 》 注释 Notes

午饭以后,他睡午觉 He takes a nap after lunch.

"睡午觉"的意思是中午吃完午饭以后睡一会儿觉,休息一下儿。
The expression "睡午觉" means to take a rest after lunch.

四 汉字知识 About Chinese Characters

偏旁：扌、门　Radical: "扌" and "门"

1. **扌**
   提手旁
   tíshǒupáng

   用在字的左边，是由"手"字变化来的。提手旁的字主要都与手的动作有关。如："打、找"。
   Radical "扌" is diverted from character "手". It is used as the left component of a character, mainly related to the action of the hand. For example: "打，找".

2. **门**
   门字框
   ménzìkuàng

   用在字的外部，带门字框的字一般与门户有关。如："阅、间"。
   Radical "门" is used as the outside component of a character. Characters with radical "门" have the meaning connected with doors. For example: "阅，间".

五 语法 Grammar

（一）动词重叠 Gemination of verbs

汉语中的不少动词可以重叠使用，单音节动词重叠时，形式为"AA"，如"看看""听听"，这时第二个音节读作轻声，即"kànkan""tīngting"；双音节动词重叠时，形式为"ABAB"，如"学习学习""研究研究"，这时第一个音节重读，第三个音节次重，第二、四个音节轻读。

Many verbs can be used reduplicatively in a sentence. The reduplicative form for monosyllabic verbs is AA, such as "看看" and "听听", and the second syllable is in the neutral tone, i.e. "kànkan" and "tīngting". The reduplicative form for disyllabic verbs is ABAB, such as "学习学习" and "研究研究". The first syllable is stressed, and the third one is a secondary stress. The 2nd and 4th syllables are in the neutral tone.

动词重叠常表示动作时间短，或动作的持续或重复，也可以表示经常性的或没有确定时间的动作，这时句子常带有轻松、随便的意味。如：

The reduplication of verbs implies that the action is short and quick, or that the action is continuous or repeated. It also means frequently-happened actions or actions without definite time. It expresses a sense of being light and relaxed. For example:

(1) 你试试这件衣服。

(2) 你帮我看看我写的汉字对不对。

(3) 太累了，你快休息休息吧。

(4) 明天我们一起去逛逛商场吧。

（二）"呢"和省略问句　"呢" and the elliptical sentence

"呢"有很多意义和用法，我们介绍如下三种。其中前两种我们已经学习过了，本课学习第三种。

The word "呢" can be used in various ways and with many meanings. The following three usages are introduced here, among which the first two have already been studied, so only the third one is studied in this lesson.

1. 表示疑问，可以用于是非问句以外的问句。如：

It means interrogative, which can be used in questions except Yes or No questions. For example:

(1) 我们怎么去呢?

(2) 这句话是谁说的呢?

2. 单用，或与"正在、正、在"前后呼应，表示正在进行的动作或行为。如：

It is used independently, or used together with "正在，正" and "在" as a corresponding, implying the action is in progress. For example:

(1) 你做什么呢?

(2) 我正在看电视呢。

3. 在一定的语言环境里，在代词、名词或名词性短语及动词短语等后面直接加上语气助词"呢"，构成疑问句"……，N 呢"，这种句子所问的内容，要由上下文来决定。如：

In the certain context, "呢" is directly added to the end of a pronoun, a noun, a noun phrase and a verb phrase, so as to form an interrogative sentence "……, N 呢", of which the content depends on the context. For example:

(1) 我是中国人，你呢？（我是中国人，你是哪国人？）

(2) 我下午去图书馆，你呢？（我下午去图书馆，你去哪儿？）

在没有上下文的情况下，这种句子一般是询问某人或某物在什么地方。如：
Without the context, this kind of structure usually inquires where somebody or something is. For example:

(1) 我的笔呢？（我的笔在哪儿？）

(2) 波伟呢？（波伟在哪儿？）

（三）号码的读法　Reading of numbers

号码中的数字不管有多少位，都要一个一个地读出。如：
Serial numbers, such as the number of a telephone, room or vehicle, must be read one by one, whether it is long or short. For example:

电话号码：　8 3 4 0 3 6 9 8　（bā sān sì líng sān liù jiǔ bā）

房间号码：　6号楼7楼 7 0 2 5 房间　（qī líng èr wǔ）

汽车牌号：　京 AW 3 6 0 8　（sān liù líng bā）

另外，如身份证号码、护照号码、门牌号码等也这样读。还要注意：
Besides, the digits in an ID number, passport number or a doorplate number are also read in the same way. What's more, the following should also be considered:

1. 号码中的"一"常读作"yāo"。如：
   "1" in a serial number is read "yāo". For example:
   报警电话110，读作：yāo yāo líng

2. 号码中的"二"读作"èr"，不能读作"liǎng"。如：
   "2" in a serial number is read "èr", not "liǎng". For example:
   急救电话120，读作：yāo èr líng

3. 号码中紧挨着的相同的数字要分别读出。如：

When there are two or more same numbers in succession, every number must be read out. For example:

火警电话119，读作：yāo yāo jiǔ

（四）时刻表达法　Reading of time-tables

汉语表达时刻的词语是："点（钟）、分、刻、半"等，口语中有时"分"可省略。如："点（钟），分，刻，半" are the words used in the expressions of time. "分" can be omitted in the oral Chinese. For example:

6:00	六点（钟）
6:05	六点零五（分）
6:10	六点十分
6:15	六点十五（分）/ 六点一刻
6:30	六点三十（分）/ 六点半
6:45	六点四十五（分）/ 六点三刻 / 差一刻七点
6:55	六点五十五（分）/ 差五分七点

询问时刻时说"现在几点"。如：
"现在几点" is the way to inquire time. For example:

A：现在几点？

B：现在八点四十。

询问动作的时间，说"……几点 + V"。如：
"……几点 + V" is used to ask the time of an action. For example:

A：明天几点出发？

B：九点出发。

六 》 重点词语 Key Words

副词"大概" Adverb "大概"

本课中的"大概"是副词,后加表示数量或时间的词语,表示对数量或时间等的不很精确的估计。如:

"大概" is an adverb in this lesson. It is used before a numeral word or a time word, meaning that one is not quite sure of the exact number or time. For example:

(1) 我们的老师大概三十岁。

(2) 我大概明年七月回国。

七 》 练 习 Exercises

(一) 朗读下面的短语 Read the following phrases

看看书	听听歌	上上网	玩儿玩儿电脑
散散步	聊聊天儿	复习复习课文	预习预习生词
发微信	看新闻	听歌	听音乐
出去吃饭	出去玩儿	开始学习	开始上课
九点十分	差一刻六点	晚上七点半	三点钟
大概三点	大概五十岁	大概下周末	大概明年四月

(二) 替换练习 Substitutions

1. A:你周末常常做什么?   休息休息

   B:我常常<u>看看电视</u>。   做做饭

   　　　　　　　　　　　　洗洗 (xǐ, wash) 衣服

   　　　　　　　　　　　　做做作业 (zuòyè, homework)

   　　　　　　　　　　　　写写汉字

   　　　　　　　　　　　　锻炼锻炼身体

2. A：我回宿舍，你呢？
   B：我去教室。

是中国人	是韩国人
晚上做作业	看电视
周末出去玩儿	在家休息

3. A：现在几点？
   B：八点。

   七点四十

   十点一刻

   差五分十二点

   两点差一刻

4. A：你们几点上课？
   B：八点。

你	起床	六点半
晚会	开始	七点
爸爸	上班	九点
妈妈	回家	五点半

5. A：你晚上做什么？
   B：有时候看电视，有时候学汉语。

几点睡觉	十一点	十二点
在哪儿吃午饭	在食堂	在宿舍
怎么去学校	骑车	坐车
工作忙吗	忙	不忙

（三）选词填空　Choose and fill in the blanks

新闻　　上网　　打球　　操场

1. 下课以后我去 _____ 锻炼身体。
2. 我常常晚上在家里 _____ 看新闻。
3. 今天电视上有什么 _____ ？
4. 你喜欢 _____ 吗？

发　　平常　　练习　　点钟

1. 这一课的 _____ 容易吗？

2. 我给妈妈 _____ 微信。

3. 爸爸 _____ 不在家，周末在家。

4. 你是不是八 _____ 上课？

（四）用"……呢"提问并回答　Ask questions with "……呢" and answer the questions

例 A：我是韩国人，你呢？

　　B：我是日本人。

1. A：安德喝茶，_____？

   B：我 _____。

2. A：我爸爸工作很忙，_____？

   B：我爸爸 _____。

3. A：我周末十点起床，_____？

   B：我 _____。

4. A：我们班有 19 个学生，_____？

   B：我们班 _____。

5. A：丁荣的自行车是蓝色的，_____？

   B：李明爱的自行车 _____。

（五）读出下面的号码或时间　Read the following numbers or time

1221 房间　　　　　214 教室　　　　　13951901748　　　83599247

京 A6978　　　　　京 B4531　　　　　新 BLA007

北京路（lù, street）　　122 号南山宾馆（bīnguǎn, hotel）503 房间

5:45　　7:08　　9:30　　10:00　　11:55　　1:30　　3:15　　4:36

（六）改错 Correct the following sentences

1. 我经常去去超市买东西。

2. 我们一起打球打球吧。

3. 我给你们介绍介绍一下王老师。

4. 我正在读读课文呢。

5. 我们明天去公园八点。

6. 我打电话妈妈明天下午三点。

（七）连词成句 Make sentences with the given words

1. 我　留学生　住　宿舍楼　312 房间
   _____

2. 每天　到　我的同屋　很早　教室
   _____

3. 他　下午五点　跑步　每天　大概　出去
   _____

4. 喜欢　我　周末　在　宿舍　睡觉
   _____

5. 六点半　我　起床　打算　明天
   _____

6. 操场　……的时候　我　跑步　去　没有课
   _____

（八）根据提示词语，看图写句子　　Make sentences according to the given words and pictures

复习　　　　电脑　　　　音乐　　　　起床　　　　跑步

（九）用下列偏旁写出至少三个汉字　　Write out at least three characters with the following radicals

扌：_____　　　门：_____

（十）描写汉字　　Trace the following characters

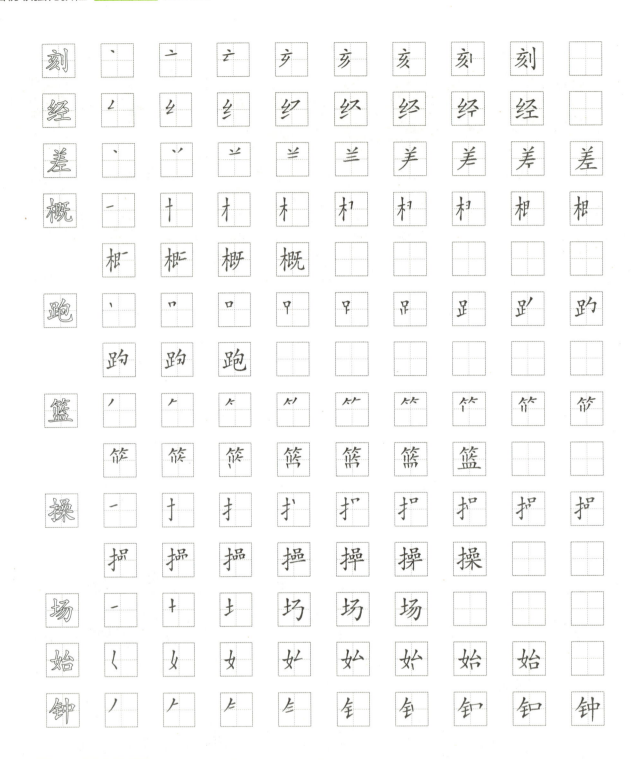

文化小贴士 Proverb

jì lái zhī, zé ān zhī.
既来之，则安之。

Now that you have been here, do as it requires.

第十七课
地铁站在哪儿

Lesson 17

Where is the subway station

这一课你将学到

语法项目 Grammar

1. 存在句：

   ……在……　　地铁站在哪儿？
   ……有……　　学校里面有书店。
   ……是……　　马路南边是华联超市。

2. 方位词：操场在体育馆后边。

3. 相邻的两个数字表示概数：七八百米

4. 又……又……：那儿的书又多又便宜。

重点词语 Key Words

1. 介词"往"：到红绿灯那儿往左拐。

2. 介词"离"：银行离学校不远。

3. 副词"就"(1)：地铁站就在那儿。

功能项目 Activity

问路

一 生词 New Words

1.	附近	n.	fùjìn	nearby
2.	边	n.	biān	side
	东边	n.	dōngbian	east
	西边	n.	xībian	west
	南边	n.	nánbian	south
	北边	n.	běibian	north
	前边	n.	qiánbian	front
	里边	n.	lǐbian	inside
	外边	n.	wàibian	outside
3.	离	prep.	lí	be away from
4.	走	v.	zǒu	walk, go, leave
5.	门口	n.	ménkǒu	entrance, doorway, gate
6.	一直	adv.	yìzhí	straight
7.	往	prep.	wǎng	towards, to
8.	灯	n.	dēng	lamp, lantern, light
	红绿灯	n.	hónglǜdēng	traffic light
9.	拐	v.	guǎi	turn, change direction
10.	马路	n.	mǎlù	road, street, avenue
11.	又	adv.	yòu	again, and, in addition
12.	体育馆	n.	tǐyùguǎn	gym, stadium
13.	米	m.(n.)	mǐ	meter
14.	寄	v.	jì	send, post, mail
15.	快递	n.	kuàidì	express

16.	刚	adv.	gāng	just
17.	方便	adj.	fāngbiàn	convenient
18.	下载	v.	xiàzài	download
19.	下单		xià dān	place an order
20.	填	v.	tián	fill in
21.	地址	n.	dìzhǐ	address
22.	预约	v.	yùyuē	reserve, make an appointment
23.	取件		qǔ jiàn	collect a porcel, pick-up
24.	服务	v./n.	fúwù	serve; service

专名 Proper Nouns

1.	华联超市	Huálián Chāoshì	BHG, Hualian Supermarket
2.	新街口	Xīnjiēkǒu	Xinjiekou Street
3.	上海	Shànghǎi	Shanghai

本课新字 New Characters

二　课文 Texts

（一）地铁站在哪儿

安德：波伟，学校附近有地铁站吗？我不知道地铁站在哪儿？

波伟：有，就在离学校不远的一家超市的西边。

安德：哪个超市？怎么走？

波伟：你从学校门口一直往北走，到红绿灯那儿往左拐，马路南边有个华联超市，地铁站在超市旁边。

安德：好的，谢谢。

波伟：安德，你去哪儿？

安德：我去新街口买书。

波伟：学校里边就有一个书店，那儿的书又多又便宜。

安德：是吗？在哪儿？

波伟：在体育馆东边，宿舍楼西边。

安德：离这儿远吗？

波伟：不远，大概有七八百米吧。

安德：谢谢，我现在就去看看。

（二）我给朋友寄快递

朋友生日快到了，他在上海，我打算给他寄一个礼物过去。但是我刚来中国，不知道怎么寄快递，于是去问波伟。他告诉我在中国寄快递很方便，可以在手机上下载一个APP，然后在APP上下单就可以。

于是，我先下载了一个快递公司的APP，然后填上了自己的姓名、电话和地址，最后预约了一个取件服务。二十分钟后，快递员就到了，他拿走了快递。他说，快递明天就能送到。我太开心了！在中国，寄快递真方便。

三 注释 Notes

我不知道怎么寄快递。 I don't know how to send express mail.

"怎么寄快递"这一小句在句子中充当句子成分。如：

The clause, in this sentence is regarded as an element of the sentence. For example:

(1) 我不知道她叫什么名字。

(2) 他说这个地址不对。

四 汉字知识 About Chinese Characters

偏旁：扌、彳　Radical: "扌" and "彳"

1. 土　提土旁 títǔpáng

用在字的左边，提土旁的字一般与泥土有关。如："地、址"。
It is used as the left component of a character. This kind of characters has a connection with earth. For example: "地，址".

2. 彳　双人旁 shuāngrénpáng

用在字的左边，双人旁的字一般与行为、动作、趋向有关。如："往、行"。
Double-person radical "彳" is used as the left component of a character, meaning performance, action or tendency. For example: "往，行".

五 语法 Grammar

（一）存在句　Existential sentences

存在句是表示人或事物存在的句子。存在句的主要作用是对客观环境进行描述，因此存在句是描写性的，不是叙述性的。

The existential sentence implies the existence of somebody or something. It mainly describes the objective situation, so it is descriptive, not narrative.

存在的几种表达方式：

There are several expressions:

1. 用"在"表示人或事物所处的方位。

"在" is used to imply the position of somebody or something.

名词（表示人或事物）	+	在	+	方位词 / 处所词
noun (sb. or sth.)	+	在	+	noun of locality
医院		在		学校旁边。
妈妈		在		爸爸左边。

2. 用"有"表示处所存在着人或事物。

"有" is used to express the existence of someone or something in the place.

方位词 / 处所词	+	有	+	名词（表示人或事物）
noun of locality	+	有	+	noun (sb. or sth.)
桌子上		有		一本书。
学校里		有		一个书店。

3. 当知道某地方有某人或某物，要求确指某人或某物是"谁"是"什么"时，用"是"。

If it is known that sb. or sth. is in a certain place, and it is must be clarified "who" or "what", "是" (be) ought to be used.

方位词 / 处所词	+	是	+	名词（表示人或事物）
noun of locality	+	是	+	noun (sb. or sth.)
宿舍前边		是		食堂。
波伟后边		是		安德。

(二) 方位词　　Nouns of locality

方位词是指表示方向和相对位置关系的名称的词。方位词又可以分为单纯方位词和合成方位词。单纯方位词如：东、南、西、北、上、下、前、后、左、右、里、外、旁等。

Nouns of locality are nouns indicating direction or position. They can be classified into monosyllabic ones and dissyllabic ones. East, south, west, north, up(top), down (bottom), front, back, left, right, inside, outside, beside and so on are the monosyllabic ones words.

合成方位词见下表（"+"表示能组合，"-"表示不能组合）：

The following form presents the dissyllabic ones （"+" means they "can" be used together and "-" means "cannot"）.

	东	南	西	北	上	下	前	后	左	右	里	外	旁
边	+	+	+	+	+	+	+	+	+	+	+	+	+
面	+	+	+	+	+	+	+	+	+	+	+	+	-

合成方位词在句中可以充当主语、宾语、定语、状语。如：

The monosyllabic noun of locality can be used as a subject, object, attributive and adverbial adjunct. For example:

(1) 外面有个老师。

(2) 银行在超市西边。

(3) 上边的书是我的。

(4) 老师，请您里边坐一会儿。

合成方位词修饰名词时，后边一般要加"的"。如：

When words of locality servers as attributives, "的" is used. For example:

旁边的学生　　左边的教室　　北面的楼　　里边的书

在国名和地名后边，不能用"里"。如：

However, "里" cannot be used after nouns indicating the geographical units. For example:

*中国里　　*南京里

（三）相邻的两个数字表示概数 Two adjacent numerals are used together to mean an approximate number

汉语用相邻的两个数词连用表示概数。如：

Two adjacent numerals are used together to mean an approximate number. For example:

七八个　　十二三斤　　一二百人

相邻的两个数词如果是十以上的，第二个数词只说它的个位数。如：

If the two adjacent numerals are over ten, only the single digit of 2nd numeral is used. For example:

十二三斤　　　　我们不说：　　*十二十三斤

二十三四岁　　　我们不说：　　*二十三二十四岁

（四）又……又…… As well as, and

"又……又……"连接并列的形容词、动词或形容词短语、动词短语，表示两种情况同时存在。如：

The structure "又……又……" is used to connect two adjectives, verbs or adjective phrases or verb phrases. It means the two situations exist at the same time. For example:

(1) 这个西瓜又大又甜（tián, sweet）。

(2) 这个孩子又哭又闹，爸爸妈妈也没有办法。

注意：我们不说"*又很高又很大"或者"*又高高的又大大的"。
Note: We cannot say "*又很高又很大" or "*又高高的又大大的".

六》 重点词语 Key Words

（一）介词"往""离" Prepositions "往" and "离"

介词"往""离"和方位词及处所词一起放在动词前做状语，表示动作行为的方向、距离等。如：

Prepositions such as "往" and "离" can be used together with nouns of locality as adverbial adjuncts before verbs, meaning the direction of an action, or the distance. For example:

表示动作方向：往+方位词/处所词

(1) 从这儿往北走。

(2) 你向前一直走，往左拐。

表示距离：离+处所词

(1) 北京离南京900多千米。

(2) 我家离他家很近。

（二）副词"就"（1）　　Adverb "就"（1）

副词"就"可以表示加强肯定。如：
Adverb "就" can be used to indicate a strong affirmation. For example:

(1) 这儿就是我们学校。

(2) 我家就在那个公园的西边。

七　练习　Exercises

（一）朗读下面的短语　Read the following phrases

往左拐	往右坐	往前看	往后走
一直走	一直看	六七百米	二三十个
从东边来	从学校走	离学校不远	离银行很远
马路北边	学校南边	我家旁边	宿舍附近
前边是宿舍	后边是安德	旁边有饭馆儿	附近有咖啡馆
又唱又跳	又吃又喝	又大又好	又便宜又好吃
我就住这儿	他就是王老师	中国北京	中国上海

（二）替换练习　Substitutions

1. A：宿舍在哪儿？
   B：在图书馆南边。

超市	东边
食堂	北边
书店	西边
操场	前边

2. A：学校里边有银行吗？
   B：有。

宿舍旁边	操场
学校外边	饭馆儿
桌子上	汉语书
楼下	超市

3. A：学校东边是什么地方？
   B：学校东边是一个书店。

右边	医院
前边	超市
后边	饭店
旁边	公园

4. A：食堂的饭菜怎么样？
   B：又好吃又便宜。

你的宿舍	大	舒服
你们的教室	干净	漂亮
她学习	努力	认真
她的衣服	好看	便宜

（三）完成对话　Complete the dialogues

1. A：地铁站在哪儿？
   B：_____。

2. A：书店在哪儿？
   B：_____。

3. A：请问，哪儿有超市？

   B：_____。

4. A：咖啡馆离酒吧远吗？

   B：_____。

5. A：那个公园怎么样？

   B：_____。

（四）选词填空　Fill in the blanks with the given words

附近　　寄　　告诉　　地铁

1. 昨天，波伟 _____ 我一件有意思的事儿。

2. 我家离学校有点儿远，我每天坐 _____ 到学校。

3. 妈妈打算一会儿去 _____ 个快递。

4. 这儿 _____ 就有一个大商场，你不用去市中心。

从……到……　　往　　离　　又……又……　　一直

1. _____ 前走一百米，马路左边就是商场。

2. _____ 北京 _____ 上海有多远？

3. 下课以后，波伟 _____ 坐在教室里看书。

4. 这家商店的东西 _____ 多 _____ 便宜。

5. 教室 _____ 宿舍很近，我每天七点半起床。

（五）选择填空　Multiple choices

1. _____ 这儿往前走，到红绿灯往右拐。

   A. 离　　　　B. 从　　　　C. 到　　　　D. 在

2. 波伟前边 _____ 丁荣。

   A. 有　　　　B. 在　　　　C. 到　　　　D. 是

3. 学校里边 _____ 咖啡馆、书店和超市。

   A. 有　　　　B. 在　　　　C. 到　　　　D. 是

4. 图书馆就 _____ 宿舍东边。

　　A. 有　　　　B. 在　　　　C. 到　　　　D. 是

5. _____ 这儿 _____ 学校有5站路。

　　A. 离　　　　B. 从　　　　C. 到　　　　D. 在

6. 请你填 _____ 自己的姓名和电话。

　　A. 从　　　　B. 往　　　　C. 上　　　　D. 在

7. 去火车站 _____ 前走，在第一个红绿灯那儿 _____ 右拐。

　　A. 从　　　　B. 往　　　　C. 到　　　　D. 离

8. 中国 _____ 你们国家远吗？

　　A. 从　　　　B. 离　　　　C. 和　　　　D. 往

（六）连词成句　Make sentences with the given words

1. 市中心　不太远　离　我们学校

　　_____

2. 就　图书馆　宿舍的东边　在

　　_____

3. 上边的　本子　桌子　我的　是

　　_____

4. 中国　在　快递　寄　方便　很

　　_____

5. 咖啡馆　里边的　便宜　好喝　又……又……　咖啡

　　_____

（七）阅读理解　Reading comprehension

　　我很喜欢我们的学校，我们的学校又大又漂亮。学校里有很多花草树木，春天 (chūntiān, spring) 的时候很美。学校很大，里面有很多楼，比如宿舍楼、办公楼、教学楼什么的，还有图书馆、操场、超市、书店、医院、食堂和一家小银行。办公楼离宿舍楼不远,就在宿舍楼西边。办公楼南边是大操场,每天都有很多人在操场上锻炼身体,我有空儿的时候也去跑步、打球。办公楼的旁边还有一个大超市,晚饭以后我们常常去超市逛逛。图书馆在操场的西边,图书馆从早上到晚上都有很多人在看书。操场的东边是银行和食堂,银行在食堂的北边,不太大,人也不太多。银行和食堂的旁边是医院,医院在书店南边,离书店大概有二三百米。

1. 根据短文判断正误　Judge the following statements according to the passage

    (1) 我们的学校不大,但是很漂亮。　　　　　　(　　)

    (2) 办公楼的西边是宿舍楼。　　　　　　　　　(　　)

    (3) 晚饭以后我们常常去逛超市。　　　　　　　(　　)

    (4) 医院在书店北边。　　　　　　　　　　　　(　　)

2. 根据短文回答问题　Answer the questions according to the passage

    (1) 学校里面都有什么?

    (2) 办公楼在哪儿?

    (3) 超市在哪儿?我们常常什么时候逛超市?

    (4) 医院在哪儿?医院离书店有多远?

(八) 看图造句　Make sentences according to the given words and pictures

寄

拐

离

填

走

（九）用下列偏旁写出至少三个汉字 Write out at least three characters with of the following radicals

土：_____

彳：_____

（十）描写汉字 Trace the following characters

文化小贴士 Proverb

Sān rén xíng bì yǒu wǒ shī.
三人行必有我师。

Even when walking in a party of no more than three,
I can always be certain of learning from those I am with.

第十八课
我不会画画儿

Lesson 18
I can not draw a picture

这一课你将学到

语法项目 Grammar

1. 能愿动词（1）：会、能、可以

   我不会画画儿。

   你能教我画画儿吗？

   我可以和你一起去。

2. 状态补语（1）

   丁荣画儿画得不错。

重点词语 Key Words

1. 副词"才"（1）

   我今天十一点才起床。

2. 副词"就"（2）

   她十几岁就开始学做饭了。

3. 介词"对"（1）

   你对画画儿感兴趣？

功能项目 Activity

商量

一 生词 New Words

1.	会	*aux.*	huì	can, be able to
2.	才	*adv.*	cái	just
3.	睡	*v.*	shuì	sleep
4.	还	*adv.*	hái	still, yet
5.	困	*adj.*	kùn	sleepy
6.	展览	*v.*	zhǎnlǎn	exhibit
7.	能	*aux.*	néng	can, be able to
8.	对	*prep.*	duì	in, to
9.	感兴趣		gǎn xìngqù	be interested in
	兴趣	*n.*	xìngqù	interest
10.	得	*part.*	de	structure particle used between a verb and its complement to indicate possibility
11.	跟	*prep.*	gēn	with, to, from, towards
12.	学	*v.*	xué	learn, study
13.	听说	*v.*	tīngshuō	hear from
14.	哪里	*pron.*	nǎli	used when responding politely to compliment
15.	大家	*pron.*	dàjiā	all of us, all, everybody
16.	爱好	*n.*	àihào	hobby
17.	了解	*v.*	liǎojiě	understand, comprehend
18.	文化	*n.*	wénhuà	civilization, culture
19.	特别	*adv.*	tèbié	particularly, special
20.	运动	*v./ n.*	yùndòng	do sports; sport
21.	踢	*v.*	tī	kick, play (football)
22.	足球	*n.*	zúqiú	football

23.	排球	n.	páiqiú	volleyball
24.	最后	n.	zuìhòu	finally
25.	尝	v.	cháng	taste

本课新字 New Characters

才　困　展　感　趣　跟　了　解　特
别　运　动　踢　足　球　排　最　尝

二　课文 Texts

（一）我不会画画儿

波伟：Āndé, qǐ chuáng ba!
安德，起床吧！

安德：Zuótiān wǎnshang wǒ liǎng diǎn cái shuì, xiànzài hái hěn kùn. Nǐ zhǎo wǒ yǒu shénme shìr?
昨天晚上我两点才睡，现在还很困。你找我有什么事儿？

波伟：Xiàwǔ yǒu ge Zhōngguóhuà zhǎnlǎn, nǐ néng hé wǒ yìqǐ qù kàn ma?
下午有个中国画展览，你能和我一起去看吗？

安德：Hǎo de, wǒ xiàwǔ méi kè, kěyǐ hé nǐ yìqǐ qù. Bōwěi, nǐ duì huàhuàr gǎn xìngqù?
好的，我下午没课，可以和你一起去。波伟，你对画画儿感兴趣？

波伟：Duì, dànshì wǒ bú huì huà.
对，但是我不会画。

安德：丁荣画儿画得不错，你可以跟她学。

波伟：是吗？我去问问她。

波伟：丁荣，听说你画儿画得很好，能教教我吗？

丁荣：哪里，我画得不好。

波伟：大家都说你画得很不错，你教教我吧。

丁荣：好。

波伟：你什么时候有空儿？

丁荣：星期一下午我有时间，可以教你，怎么样？

波伟：好的。下个星期一我来找你。

（二）我们的爱好

昨天上课的时候，老师问我们有什么爱好。波伟说他对画画儿很感兴趣，但是不会画，丁荣说可以教他，波伟很高兴。丁荣的爱好是画画儿，她觉得画画儿很有意思。她现在也很喜欢中国画，她觉得学习中国画可以了解中国文化。安德特别喜欢运动，踢足球、打排球、打羽毛球，他都非常喜欢。李明爱的爱好很有趣，她喜欢做饭，她说她饭做得很好吃。她告诉大家她很早就开始学做饭，所以，饭做得非常好。最后，她还请大家有空儿的时候去尝尝她做的饭菜，大家都很高兴。

三 注释 Notes

哪里。 You flatter me!

用在被别人称赞的时候，表示谦虚，意思是"不是"。也可以说"哪里，哪里"。又如：

"哪里" is a modest response to others' praise, and the meaning is: You flatter me, I am not deserve the praise. For example:

(1) A：你的汉语说得真好。

B：哪里，说得不好。

(2) A：你这件衣服真漂亮。

B：哪里哪里，一般。

四 汉字知识 About Chinese Characters

偏旁：忄、⺮　　Radicals: "忄" and "⺮"

1.
竖心旁
shùxīnpáng

用在字的左边，竖心旁的字一般与思想有关。如："快、懂"。
Radical "忄" is used as the left component of a character, implying mind or thought. For example: "快，懂".

2.
竹字头
zhúzìtóu

用在字的上边，带竹字头的字一般与竹子有关。如："笔、筷"。
Radical "⺮" is used as the top component of a character, implying bamboo. For example: "笔，筷".

五 语法 Grammar

（一）能愿动词（1）　Modal verbs (1)

能愿动词是表示意愿、要求、可能、准许等的动词。大多数能愿动词可以单独做谓语。可以用肯定、否定并列的形式表示疑问。可以受某些副词修饰，不可以重叠。

Modal verbs are the verbs to express willings, requirements, possibilities or permissions. Most of modal verbs can be used as a predicate independently. Combination of affirmative and negative forms can express interrogation. They can be modified by some adverbs, but a modal verb cannot be reduplicated.

1. 表示可能的能愿动词有"能"和"会"等。
Modal verbs "能" and "会" can express possibilities.

会　can, be able to, be good at

表示懂得怎样做或有能力做某事，善于做某事。否定时用"不会"。如：
It means knowing how to do or being able to do or being good at doing something. "不

会" is its negative form. For example:

(1) 我会说汉语，她会说法语。

(2) 我不会打太极拳。

能　can, be able to

表示有能力或有条件做某事，环境或情理上许可。如：

It means one is capable of doing something, or possibility provided by circumstances or reasons. For example:

(3) 他能说汉语。

(4) 对不起，我有事儿，不能和你一起去。

注意：表示主观上具有某种技能、客观上具有某种条件，用"能"，特别是只侧重于这种能力时，只能用"能"；表示通过学习或练习而掌握某种技能时用"会"。如：

Note: Modal verb "能" can be used when one has a certain skill or ability and the conditions are proper. Only "能" can express capability. Modal verb "会" can be used to express the grasp of a skill or ability through learning or practising. For example:

(5) 我喝酒了，不能开车。

我们不说：We can't say:

*我喝酒了，不会开车。

再如：More examples:

(6) 我能喝酒。

(7) 我会喝酒。

"能"是说条件允许、可以喝酒或具有喝酒的能力；"会"是说具有喝酒的能力或有喝酒的技巧。

"能" means that the situations permit sb. to drink, or sb. has the ability to drink. "会" means sb. has the ability to drink or can drink skillfully.

2. "可以"表示可能、能够或许可，意思是"能够"。否定时一般用"不能"。如：

It expresses the meaning of "can" or "be able to". The negative form is "不能".

(1) 这个房子可以住四个人。

(2) 我可以进来吗？

（3）我明天上课，不能去了。

注意："能"和"可以"都有表示"能够"的意思。但是，"能"可以表示善于做某事，而"可以"不能。如：

Note: Both of "能" and "可以" can express the meaning of "can". However, the word "能" means "be good at doing sth.", while the word "可以" has no such an implication. For example:

（4）他很能喝酒，每次都喝三四瓶。

我们不说：We can't say:

＊他很可以喝酒，每次都喝三四瓶。

"能"可以表示有某种客观的可能性，"可以"不行。如：

The word "能" means that there is a certain kind of objective possibility, but the word "可以" has no such an implication. For example:

（5）这么晚他还能来吗？

我们不说：We can't say:

＊这么晚他还可以来吗？

在结构上，"可以"能单独做谓语，"能"一般不这样用。如：

"可以" can be as the predicate independently, but "能" has no such an implication. For example:

（6）这样做也可以。

我们不说：We can't say:

＊这样做也能。

（二）状态补语（1）　State complement (1)

状态补语是动词后用"得"连接的表示动作结果、状态等的补语。它的主要功能是对动作进行描写、评价和判断。

State complement is a complement following a verb by "得", indicating the result or state of the verb. Its main function is to describe, judge or evaluate on the verb actions.

肯定式　Positive form:

		动词	得	形容词
		verb	得	adjective
他	太极拳	打	得	很好。
丁荣	汉语	说	得	不错。
妹妹	画儿	画	得	很不错。

动词带有宾语时，需重复动词：
The verb must to be repeated when it takes an object:

动词	宾语	动词	得	形容词
verb	object	verb	得	adjective
他	说	汉语	说	得	很好。
她	画	画儿	画	得	不错。

在交际中，我们经常会省略第一个动词，这时句子就变成了主谓谓语句。如：
In communication, the first verb is usually omitted, thus, the sentence structure becomes the sentence with a subject-predicate phrase as the predicate.

(1) 他汉语说得好。

(2) 她画儿画得不错。

否定式　Negative form:

	动词	得	不	形容词
	verb	得	不	adjective
我汉字	写	得	不	太好。
她汉语	说	得	不	好。

正反疑问句　Affirmative-negative questions:

	动词	得	形容词	不	形容词
	verb	得	adjective	不	adjective
她汉语	说	得	好	不	好？
他画儿	画	得	好看	不	好看？

六 重点词语 Key Words

（一）副词"才"（1） Adverb "才"（1）

副词"才"在这里表示事情发生或结束得晚。前面有时会有表示时间晚、历时长的词语。如：

Adverb "才" means something occurs or ends late. Sometimes, time word of expressing "late" or "long" is added before "才". For example:

(1) 他晚上十二点才睡。

(2) 他明天才能到。

（二）副词"就"（2） Adverb "就"（2）

副词"就"在这里强调事情发生得早。"就"前应有时间词语或其他副词。

Adverb "就" emphasizes the earliness of an act. Time words or other adverbs should be placed before "就". For example:

(1) 我四岁就开始学习英语。

(2) 我从小就喜欢看书。

（三）介词"对"（1） Preposition "对"（1）

介词"对"后加名词、代词，构成介宾短语做状语。如：

The preposition "对", together with the nouns or pronouns following it, forms a prepositional phrase as an adverbial adjunct. For example:

(1) 我对中国文化很感兴趣。

(2) 对这个问题，大家都很感兴趣。

七 练习 Exercises

（一）朗读下面的短语　Read the following phrases

会写汉字	不会说汉语	会不会听	会不会做
能做饭	不能开车	能不能看	能不能说
可以看书	不能说话	可以不可以唱歌	可以不可以听音乐
打得不错	画得很好	写得很漂亮	睡得不早
做得不错	听得不对	教得不好	唱得好听
很晚才回来	八点才上课	五点就开始	很早就走

（二）替换练习　Substitutions

1. A：你会唱<u>中文歌</u>吗？
   B：不会。

   写汉字
   跳舞
   做饭
   游泳（yóu yǒng, swim）

2. A：你下午能和我一起去<u>银行</u>吗？
   B：对不起，我下午去<u>看病</u>。

   图书馆　　教室
   超市　　　公司
   买书　　　买衣服

3. A：可以<u>坐</u>吗？
   B：对不起，不行。

   抽烟（chōu yān, smoke）
   唱歌
   听音乐
   打电话

4. A：他(说)汉语 说得怎么样?
   B：很好。

(做)饭	做	好吃
(打)球	打	不错
(唱)歌	唱	好听
(写)汉字	写	漂亮

（三）看图造句　Make sentences according to the given words and pictures

不会　画画儿

一起　看展览

教　画画儿

做饭　很好

两点　才睡

（四）选词填空　Fill in the blanks with the given words

画　　了解　　感兴趣　　会　　能

1. 你为什么对中国文化 _____ ?

2. 她 _____ 画儿 _____ 得很不错。

3. 我才来中国两天，还不 _____ 说汉语。

4. 多看看介绍中国的书可以帮助我们 _____ 中国文化。

5. 喝酒以后不 _____ 开车。

得　　可是　　跟　　才　　就

1. 那个画展很不错，_____ 我今天有课，不能和你一起去。

2. 她做饭做得很好吃，你 _____ 她学学。

3. 我们十点见面，他九点 _____ 到了。

4. 他昨天晚上喝酒喝 _____ 不太多。

5. 我们国家离中国很远，三天 _____ 能到家。

（五）选择填空　Multiple choices

1. 我不是法国人，我不 _____ 说法语。
   A．得　　　B．行　　　C．会　　　D．可以

2. 她一分钟 _____ 写二十个汉字。
   A．得　　　B．不会　　C．会　　　D．能

3. 对不起，这儿不 _____ 游泳。
   A．行　　　B．能　　　C．会　　　D．要

4. 这件衣服不错，你 _____ 试试。
   A．可以　　B．能　　　C．会　　　D．得

5. 最近我很忙，不 _____ 来了。
   A．要　　　B．会　　　C．得　　　D．行

6. 我的自行车坏了，我 _____ 借你的自行车吗？
   A．能　　　B．要　　　C．行　　　D．会

7. 这本书你送给他也 _____ 。
   A．能　　　B．会　　　C．可以　　D．得

8. 他跳舞跳 _____ 真不错。
   A．地　　　B．的　　　C．得　　　D．很

（六）在空格里填上适当的状态补语　Fill in blanks with proper state complements

例　他的汉语说得<u>很不错</u>。

1. 波伟跑步跑得 _____ 。

2. 李明爱做饭做得 _____ 。

3. 他每天都来得_____。

4. 这个字她读得不_____。

5. 安德游泳（yóu yǒng, swim）游得_____。

（七）连词成句　Make sentences with the given words

1. 我妈妈　起得　很早　早上
_____

2. 不会　我　中国画　画
_____

3. 可以　用用　我　吗　你的笔
_____

4. 别人的　我们　看　考试的时候　不能
_____

5. 很好　你的歌　唱得　我听说
_____

（八）写作　Writing

根据所给词语和图片写一段话，不少于80字。
Write a short passage according to the pictures and given words at least 80 characters.

爱好　　感兴趣　　写　　汉字
练习　　会　　　　最后　能
了解　　中国文化

（九）用下列偏旁写出至少三个汉字　Write out at least three characters with the following radicals

忄：_____　　　　　　　　竹：_____

(十) 描写汉字　Trace the following characters

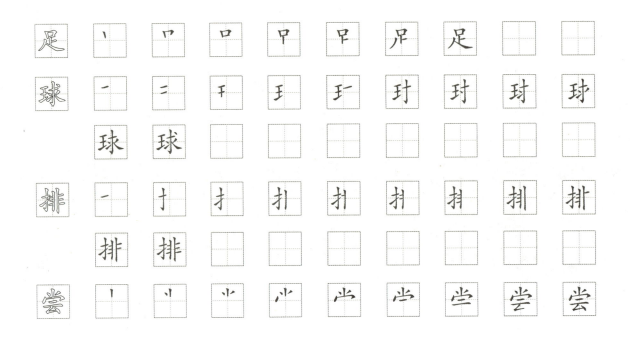

🌱 文化小贴士 Proverb

Qín néng bǔ zhuō.
勤 能 补 拙。

Clumsy can be overcome by diligence.

第十九课
我不喜欢在网上买衣服

Lesson 19

I don't like to buy clothes online

这一课你将学到

语法项目 Grammar

1. 能愿动词（2）：想、要、愿意
   我*想*买台电脑。
   你*要*买什么牌子的？
   大家都很*愿意*去那儿买东西。

2. 程度补语（1）：形容词+得很
   有名的牌子都贵*得很*。

3. 兼语句：
   他让我来你的宿舍。

4. 一边……一边……
   他*一边*笑，*一边*说。

功能项目 Activities

咨询意见、介绍商店的种类

一 生词 New Words

1.	让	v.	ràng	let
2.	马上	adv.	mǎshàng	at once, immediately
3.	懂	v.	dǒng	understand, know
4.	出	v.	chū	go out, exit, give
5.	主意	n.	zhǔyi	idea
6.	邮件	n.	yóujiàn	mail
7.	文章	n.	wénzhāng	article, essay
8.	电影	n.	diànyǐng	film, movie
9.	牌子	n.	páizi	brand
10.	有名	adj.	yǒumíng	well-known, famous
11.	咱们	pron.	zánmen	we, us
12.	前天	n.	qiántiān	the day before yesterday
13.	服装店	n.	fúzhuāngdiàn	clothing shop
14.	可是	conj.	kěshì	but, yet, however
15.	只好	adv.	zhǐhǎo	have to, have no choice but
16.	一边	adv.	yìbiān	beside, at the same time
17.	笑	v.	xiào	smile, laugh
18.	用品	n.	yòngpǐn	articles for use
19.	丰富	adj.	fēngfù	rich, abundant, plentiful
20.	而且	conj.	érqiě	and, what's more, in addition
21.	好处	n.	hǎochù	advantage, benefit
22.	觉得	v.	juéde	think
23.	样子	n.	yàngzi	style
24.	麻烦	adj.	máfan	troublesome
25.	好好儿	adv.	hǎohāor	to one's heart's content, well

26.	选	v.	xuǎn	choose
27.	退换	v.	tuìhuàn	exchange a purchase

本课新字 New Characters

让　懂　主　意　邮　章　牌　咱
服　装　只　笑　用　品　丰　富
而　且　处　觉　麻　烦　选　换

二 课文 Texts

（一）我想买台电脑

Bōwěi: Lǐ Míng'ài, Āndé shuō nǐ zhǎo wǒ, ràng wǒ mǎshàng lái nǐde sùshè.
波伟：李明爱，安德说你找我，让我马上来你的宿舍。

Lǐ Míng'ài: Shì, wǒ yǒu shìr zhǎo nǐ.
李明爱：是，我有事儿找你。

Bōwěi: shénme shìr?
波伟：什么事儿？

Lǐ Míng'ài: Wǒ xiǎng mǎi tái diànnǎo, dànshì bú tài dǒng, nǐ bāng wǒ chūchu zhúyi ba.
李明爱：我想买台电脑，但是不太懂，你帮我出出主意吧。

Bōwěi: Nǐ dàgài xiǎng mǎi duōshao qián de?
波伟：你大概想买多少钱的？

Lǐ Míng'ài: Wǔ-liù qiān kuài de ba.
李明爱：五六千块的吧。

波伟：你为什么要买电脑？

李明爱：我想用电脑上上网，发发邮件，写写文章，看看电影。

波伟：你要买什么牌子的？

李明爱：一般的吧，有名的牌子都贵得很。

波伟：名牌儿也有便宜的。你打算什么时候去买？

李明爱：我明天下午没课，想明天下午去。

波伟：要我和你一起去吗？

李明爱：我请你来，就是想让你陪我一起去啊。

波伟：好，明天下课以后，咱们一起去。

李明爱：好的，明天见。

（二）我不喜欢在网上买衣服

前天，我去学校附近的一个小服装店买衣服，可是，那儿衣服很少，我没买到合适的。我只好去离学校很远的一家大商场里买，可是那儿的衣服很贵。

回到学校以后，我告诉波伟买衣服的事儿。他一边笑，一边问我为什么不在网上买衣服。波伟说，他常常在网上买衣服、生活用品。网上的东西各式各样，丰富极了，而且价格比较便宜，在网上买东西很方便。我当然知道在网上买东西的好处。可是，我觉得在网上买衣服不能试，所以不知道大小和样子合适不合适，退换有点儿麻烦。波伟觉得不麻烦，他说买东西之前好好儿地选选，就不会退换了。

三 汉字知识 About Chinese Characters

偏旁：力、月　　Radical:"力" and "月"

1. **力**
力字旁
lìzìpáng

力字旁的字一般与力量、力气有关。如："助、动"。
Characters with radical "力" have the meaning connected with force. For example: "助,动".

2. **月**
月字旁
yuèzìpáng

用在字的左边和右边，月字旁的字一般与月亮有关。如："明、望"。
Radical "月" is used as the right or left side component of a character. Characters with this radical have the meaning connected with the moon. For example: "明,望".

四 语法 Grammar

（一）能愿动词（2） Modal verbs (2)

我们学过了表示可能、能够、准许的能愿动词。这里我们来学习一下表示意愿、要求的能愿动词。

We have learnt the modal verbs meaning possibilities, capabilities and permissions. In this lesson, we will learn some other modal verbs meaning wishes and demands.

表示愿望和意愿的能愿动词有"想""要"和"愿意"等。
Modal verbs "想,要" and "愿意" means one's will and requirement.

1. 想　wish, plan

表示愿望和打算。如：
It means a wish or a plan. For example:

(1) 我想学画画儿。

(2) 我今天不想去上课。

2．要　require, ought to

表示要求，应该做某事。否定时一般用"不想"来回答。如：

It means one is required or ought to do something. "不想" is its negative form. For example:

A：你一定要来玩儿呀。

B：我不想去玩儿。

注意："想"着重于一种愿望，是一种打算。而"要"侧重于做某事的决心，是意志上的要求。"想"前面可以受程度副词的修饰，"要"不能。"要"前面可以受"一定"等副词的修饰，"想"一般不能。如：

Note: "想" focuses on a wish or a plan, while "要" focuses on the determination or a will. "想" can be modified by an adverb of degree, while "要" cannot. "要" can be modified by adverbs such as "一定", but "想" can't be modified by some adverbs. For example:

我很想来中国学习汉语。

我们不说：We cannot say:

＊我很要来中国学习汉语。

3．愿意　will

表示做某事或发生某种情况是自己所希望的。可以受程度副词修饰。前面可以用助动词"会""能"。如：

It means that one wants to do something. It can be modified by adverbs of degree. Auxiliary verbs such as "会" and "能" can be added before it. For example:

（1）我很愿意来中国学习汉语。

（2）你愿意不愿意教我画画儿？

（3）你说我能愿意这样做吗？

（二）程度补语（1）　The complement of degree (1)

程度补语从意义上来说是表示程度的，在形式上有用"得"连接和不用"得"连接两种。程度补语一般只能与形容词和表示感情、感觉以及心理活动、心理状态的动词一起用。如：

From the aspect of significance, the complement of degree illustrates the degree of an action. There are two forms, one is connected by "得" and another is not. Usually the complement of degree can only be used together with adjectives and verbs expressing emotion, feeling, psychological activities and states. For example:

	形容词 adjective	+	得很 得很
你这件衣服	漂亮		得很。
今天	热		得很。
这台电脑	贵		得很。

（三）兼语句　Pivotal sentence

兼语句的谓语由一个动宾短语和一个主谓短语套合在一起构成，动宾短语中的宾语兼做后面主谓短语的主语。如：

The pivotal sentence means that the predicate consists of a verb-object phrase and a subject-predicate structure. The object of the first predicate is at the same time the subject of the second one. For example:

$$S_1 \quad V_1 \quad O_1$$
我　请　老师　教　语法。
$$\quad\quad\quad\quad S_2 \quad V_2 \quad O_2$$

句中"老师"兼做前一个结构的宾语和后一个结构的主语，叫作"兼语"，这种句子就叫兼语句。

In the above example, "老师" is the object of the former structure and also the subject of the later structure.

兼语句中的第一个动词多是表示使令意义的，如"使、让、叫、请、派"等，兼语后的动作或状态表明前一个动作要达到的目的、结果。如：

In this kind of sentence, the first verb is usually the imperative one, such as "使，让，叫，请，派" and so on. The action or state after the object indicates the purpose and result of the action indicated by the first verb. For example:

(1) 妈妈让我吃饭。

(2) 大家请她唱歌。

（四）一边……一边…… Beside, at the same time

表示两种以上的动作同时进行，一般用在动词前面。如：

It indicates that two or more actions are done (or in progress) simultaneously. It is used before the verbs. For example:

(1) 我妹妹一边唱，一边跳。

(2) 他一边听音乐，一边写作业。

注意："一边"中的"一"可以省略，省略"一"后，同单音节动词组合时，中间不停顿。如：

Note: The character "一" in "一边" can be omitted. After omitting, while pairing with a monosyllabic verb, there is no pause in the middle. For example:

  边说边笑 边看边写 边走边聊

"边"只用于同一主语；"一边"可以用于不同主语。如：

"边" can only be used with the same subject, while "一边" may be used with different subjects. For example:

我边看边听。

我们不说：We can't say:

*我边看，他边说。

五　练习 Exercises

（一）朗读下面的短语 Read the following phrases

想回国	想看书	不想听歌	想不想学习
想要做饭	想要学跳舞	不想去银行	要不要试试这件衣服
愿意说英语	愿意做练习	不愿意听音乐	愿意不愿意参加
说得好得很	漂亮得很	中国歌好听得很	他的字写得好得很
一边看一边写	一边听一边看	边笑边说	边走边听
老师让我们做作业		同屋让我买早饭	我让他回宿舍

（二）替换练习　Substitutions

1. A：你想去<u>看电影</u>吗？
   B：对不起，我没时间。

   看展览
   学唱歌
   去公园玩儿
   去超市买东西

2. 我要<u>去超市</u> <u>买面包</u>，不想<u>去商店买</u>。

去教室	看书	在宿舍看
去电影院	看电影	在家看
回宿舍	休息	出去玩儿
去体育馆	打排球	踢足球

3. 我不愿意吃<u>他做的菜</u>。

   学习英语
   自己做饭
   和他住在一起
   一个人去锻炼身体

4. <u>老师</u>让他唱一个中文歌。

老师	她交作业
妈妈	我在家里休息
姐姐	我给她发微信
他	我去寄个快递

5. 这<u>件</u> <u>衣服</u> <u>便宜</u>得很。

个	包	贵
个	教室	干净
双	鞋	舒服
张	桌子	大

（三）看图造句　Make sentences according to the given words and pictures

想　买电脑

愿意　那家饭馆儿

买　牌子

一边……一边……

（四）选词填空　Fill in the blanks with the given words

主意　　好处　　有名　　文章　　咱们

1. 我也不知道怎么做，你给我出个好_____吧。

2. 我很想去那个_____的大学学几年汉语。

3. 下课以后_____一起去电影院看电影吧。

4. 这篇_____写得很好，你看一看。

5. 在网上买东西有很多_____，所以我喜欢在网上买。

想　让　要　只好　一边……一边……

1. 他经常_____写作业，_____听音乐。

2. 妈妈_____小明帮她去超市买一点儿水果。

3. 波伟不知道这个字怎么读，_____问丁荣。

4. 老师让我们每天都_____努力学习。

5. 我对中国文化很感兴趣，所以我_____去中国学学汉语，了解了解中国文化。

(五) 选择填空　Multiple choices

1. 今年五月，我很 _____ 和朋友去北京玩儿。
   A．想　　　　B．愿意　　　　C．会　　　　D．能

2. 明天有考试，我们 _____ 早睡早起。
   A．愿意　　　B．会　　　　　C．能　　　　D．要

3. 他不愿意和我一起去，我 _____ 自己去。
   A．就　　　　B．只　　　　　C．所以　　　D．只好

4. 这件事你不 _____ 做没关系，我让别人做。
   A．只　　　　B．可以　　　　C．愿意　　　D．还

5. 你 _____ 明天去还是后天去？
   A．能　　　　B．会　　　　　C．想　　　　D．只

6. 妈妈让我在中国一定 _____ 好好儿学习。
   A．能　　　　B．要　　　　　C．想　　　　D．会

7. 超市的东西很便宜，_____ 也很丰富。
   A．一边　　　B．又　　　　　C．而且　　　D．还

8. 今天的电影好看 _____。
   A．非常　　　B．得很　　　　C．很　　　　D．比较

(六) 连词成句　Make sentences with the given words

1. 我　和　食堂　吃饭　想去　朋友
   _____

2. 要　我　明天下午　去医院　陪妈妈
   _____

3. 愿意　自己　我　住　不
   _____

4. 不让　我们　老师　玩儿手机　上课的时候

_____

5. 喜欢　一边　看电视　小明的妈妈　一边　吃饭

_____

(七) 阅读理解　Reading comprehension

　　我从小在北方长大（zhǎngdà, grow up），所以不会游泳。到南方上学以后，看见这里的人都会游泳，我也很想学。我问同屋怎么才能学会游泳，同屋告诉我可以参加游泳班。她说学校附近有一个体育馆，在体育馆就可以报名（bào míng, enter one's name）参加游泳班，让我去那儿看看。下课以后，我去了体育馆。报名的地方只有一个人，我告诉他我想报名学习游泳。他看看我，然后给我一张纸，让我写上自己的名字和电话。他问我想从什么时候开始学习游泳，还问我想参加晚上的班还是白天的班。我想，自己白天要上课，所以就告诉他参加晚上的班。最后，他让我交800块钱，让我一个星期以后来学游泳。

1. 根据短文判断正误　Judge the following statements according to the passage

　　(1) 我是南方人。　　　　　　　　　　　　　(　　)

　　(2) 我游泳游得不好。　　　　　　　　　　　(　　)

　　(3) 我在学校里的体育馆报名学习游泳。　　　(　　)

2. 根据短文回答问题　Answer the questions according to the passage

　　(1) 我为什么不会游泳？

　　(2) 我白天学习游泳还是晚上学习游泳？

　　(3) 游泳班在哪儿？

　　(4) 学习游泳需要交多少钱？

（八）用下列偏旁写出至少三个汉字 Write out at least three characters with the following radicals

力：_____   月：_____

（九）描写汉字 Trace the following characters

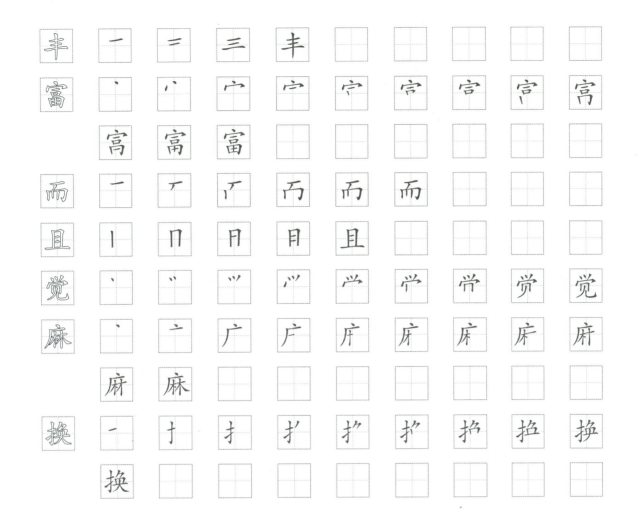

文化小贴士 Proverb

Méihuā xiāng zì kǔ hán lái.
梅花香自苦寒来。
Plum blossom smells nicer after the cold winter.

第二十课 复习（四）

Lesson 20 Review (IV)

一 ▶ 生词 New Words

1.	酒店	n.	jiǔdiàn	hotel
2.	旅行	v.	lǚxíng	travel
3.	顺便	adv.	shùnbiàn	by the way, passingly
4.	合适	adj.	héshì	suitable, appropriate
5.	周围	n.	zhōuwéi	around
6.	环境	n.	huánjìng	enviroment, surroundings
7.	片	m.	piàn	part of place
8.	排	m.	pái	row
9.	高大	adj.	gāodà	tall
10.	树木	n.	shùmù	tree
11.	花园	n.	huāyuán	garden
12.	办	v.	bàn	handle, do

270

13.	入住	v.	rùzhù	check in
14.	手续	n.	shǒuxù	procedure
15.	登记	v.	dēngjì	register, check in
16.	等	aux.	děng	and so on
17.	信息	n.	xìnxī	information, message
18.	护照	n.	hùzhào	passport
19.	价格	n.	jiàgé	price
20.	满意	v.	mǎnyì	satisfied, pleased

本课新字 New Characters

酒 店 顺 合 适 围 环 境 高
木 花 园 办 续 护 价 格 满

二 课文 Text

那家酒店很不错

Shàng ge xīngqī, bàba māma lái Zhōngguó lǚxíng. Jīntiān, tāmen cóng Shànghǎi
上 个 星期，爸爸 妈妈 来 中国 旅行。今天，他们 从 上海

zuò fēijī dào Běijīng lái kàn wǒ. Tāmen yào zài Běijīng zhù sān-sì tiān, guàngguang
坐 飞机 到 北京 来看 我。他们 要 在 北京 住 三四 天， 逛逛

Běijīng, shùnbiàn yě kànkan wǒ shēnghuó、xuéxí de dìfang. Suǒyǐ, wǒ dǎsuàn zài
北京，顺便 也 看看 我 生活、学习 的 地方。所以，我 打算 在

学校附近给他们找一家酒店。可是，我不知道哪儿有合适的酒店，就去问王明。他告诉我，从学校西门出去，往右拐，走三四百米，就有一家酒店，那家很不错。而且，有很多外国人住在那儿。

下午，我带爸爸妈妈去那家酒店。酒店周围的环境很好，门前有一大片草地，旁边有两排高大的树木，还有一个漂亮的小花园。爸爸妈妈很喜欢这儿。

进酒店后，我先去办入住手续。可是我的汉语说得不太好，于是，服务员让一个会说英语的同事给我当翻译，他的英语说得很好。服务员先登记了我们的姓名、电话等信息，然后，让我给他看看护照。手续办完了，我们就去房间了。爸爸妈妈觉得这儿离学校很近，方便得很，价格也不贵。他们对这家酒店很满意，都愿意住在那儿。

三 练习 Exercises

（一）根据课文内容判断正误　Judge the following statements true or false according to the text

1. 爸爸妈妈从国外坐飞机来看"我"。　　　　　　　　　（　　）
2. 爸爸妈妈住在"我"的宿舍里。　　　　　　　　　　　（　　）
3. "我"知道学校附近有一家很不错的酒店。　　　　　　（　　）
4. 昨天下午，"我"带爸爸妈妈去酒店办手续。　　　　　（　　）
5. 服务员的英语都很好。　　　　　　　　　　　　　　（　　）
6. "我"的汉语说得很不错。　　　　　　　　　　　　　（　　）
7. 这个酒店的价格比较便宜。　　　　　　　　　　　　（　　）
8. 爸爸妈妈对这家酒店比较满意。　　　　　　　　　　（　　）

（二）选词填空　Fill in the blanks with the given words

旅行　　环境　　登记　　情况　　周围

1. 中国又大又漂亮，我想去别的城市＿＿＿＿＿＿＿，看看美丽的风景。
2. 学校＿＿＿＿＿＿＿有饭馆儿、商店、银行，还有邮局，生活很方便。
3. 请在这里＿＿＿＿＿＿＿一下您的名字，然后您可以上楼。
4. 每个周末我都给爸爸妈妈打电话，告诉他们我最近的学习＿＿＿＿＿＿＿。
5. 学校里的＿＿＿＿＿＿＿很好，有树有花儿，还有一个漂亮的湖。

往　　可是　　离　　从　　一边……一边……

1. 我想学踢足球，＿＿＿＿＿＿＿没人愿意教我。
2. 你不要＿＿＿＿＿＿＿看书＿＿＿＿＿＿＿看电视。
3. ＿＿＿＿＿＿＿晚会开始还有半个小时，你再练习练习。
4. 去银行从这儿＿＿＿＿＿＿＿前走，到邮局那儿＿＿＿＿＿＿＿左拐。

273

5. 我们每天 _____ 八点到十二点都有课。

的　　得

1. 他们班 _____ 汉语课明天上。

2. 今天 _____ 作业，大家明天要给我。

3. 他汉字写 _____ 非常漂亮。

4. 哥哥打篮球打 _____ 很不错。

5. 桌子上 _____ 那本书是谁的？

会　　能　　想　　要　　愿意

1. 我很 _____ 去图书馆看书，不 _____ 在宿舍睡觉。

2. 你明天一定 _____ 来上课！

3. 我不 _____ 和我的同屋一起住，他常常很晚睡觉。

4. 今天波伟身体不舒服，不 _____ 来上课。

5. 他 _____ 开车，但是喝酒后不 _____ 开车。

（三）连词成句　Make sentences with the given words

1. 能　吗　让我看看　新书　你的

　_____

2. 买　早饭　帮他　让我　同屋

　_____

3. 想　玩儿　明天下午　去朋友家　我

　_____

4. 打　羽毛球　怎么样　打得　他

　_____

5. 这家酒店　对　不　满意　爸爸妈妈

　_____

（四）排列顺序　Compose a paragraph in the correct order

1. A. 上个星期，爸爸妈妈来中国旅行
   B. 他们要看看我生活和学习的地方
   C. 今天，他们从上海坐火车来北京看我　　_____

2. A. 我打算给他们在学校附近找一个酒店
   B. 就去找王明问问
   C. 但是我不知道哪儿有　　_____

3. A. 后边还有一条小河
   B. 宿舍前边有一大片草地和几排树木
   C. 学校里的环境很好　　_____

4. A. 我先去办理入住手续
   B. 然后让我给她看看护照
   C. 服务员登记了我的信息　　_____

5. A. 出去方便得很
   B. 他们觉得那儿离学校很近
   C. 价格也比较便宜　　_____

（五）阅读理解　Reading comprehension

昨天下午我和几个朋友去博物馆参观。博物馆非常大，里面的东西很多，也很好看，我们从一点看到六点，快关门的时候才出来。出来以后，我们决定（juédìng, decide）在附近的小饭馆儿吃饭。因为吃得太多，我们几个决定走走。我们一边走，一边聊天儿，最后发现回学校的路不对。我看看表，现在已经九点半了，怎么办呢？还是问问别人吧。前面有几个年轻人，我就去问他们，知道不知道回学校的路。他们很热情（rèqíng, enthusiastic），告诉我应该怎么走。接着，他们还问我为什么学汉语，他们一直说我汉语说得很好。我心里很高兴。我们一边聊一边往学校走。回到宿舍时十一点了，虽然

(suīrán, although）很晚，但是我很高兴，因为我觉得今天的收获 (shōuhuò, obtain) 很大。

1. 根据短文判断正误　Judge the following statements according to the passage

　　（1）我是和同屋去博物馆参观的。　　　　　　　　　　（　　）

　　（2）我们不喜欢坐车，所以走路回学校。　　　　　　　（　　）

　　（3）我很高兴，我觉得收获很大。　　　　　　　　　　（　　）

2. 根据短文回答问题　Answer the questions according to the passage

　　（1）博物馆可能几点关门？

　　（2）为什么我们回学校的路走得不对？

　　（3）谁告诉我们回学校的路？

（六）看图造句　Make sentences according to the given words and pictures

　　　旅行　　　　　　环境　　　　　　价格　　　　　满意

（七）写作　Writing

　　根据所给词语写一段话，不少于80字。
　　Write a short passage according to the given words at least 80 characters.

　　陪　去　医院　不知道　哪儿　离　银行　不远　一直
　　往　走　五百米　到

（八）根据偏旁给下列汉字归类 Sort the following characters according to the radicals

很　庆　住　游　服　康　忙　回　草　脑　英
得　朋　律　泳　行　应　街　洗　汉　快　菜
店　恨　法　情　床　明　慢　往　节　懒

例　彳：得　行　街　往

___ : _____　　　　___ : _____

___ : _____　　　　___ : _____

___ : _____　　　　___ : _____

___ : _____

（九）描写汉字 Trace the following characters

酒　店　合　适　围　环　境

文化小贴士 Proverb

Wù yǐ shàn xiǎo ér bù wéi, wù yǐ è xiǎo ér wéi zhī.
勿以善小而不为，勿以恶小而为之。

Do not neglect something of a little benefit, do not do something of a little sin.

生词索引

A

| 爱好 | àihào | 18 |
| 安静 | ānjìng | 9 |

B

吧	ba	8
把	bǎ	9
爸爸	bàba	10
百	bǎi	9
班	bān	7
办	bàn	20
半	bàn	11
帮助	bāngzhù	13
报纸	bàozhǐ	9
北边	běibian	17
本子	běnzi	6
比较	bǐjiào	13
笔	bǐ	6
毕业	bìyè	15
边	biān	17
别的	biéde	13
饼干	bǐnggān	11
不	bù	2
不错	búcuò	13
不用	búyòng	8

C

才	cái	18
操场	cāochǎng	16
草地	cǎodì	14
差	chà	16
尝	cháng	18
常常	chángcháng	10
唱	chàng	12
超市	chāoshì	11
城市	chéngshì	15
出	chū	19
出去	chūqù	15
出生	chūshēng	5
出租车	chūzūchē	14
词典	cídiǎn	4
从	cóng	13

D

打	dǎ	12
打算	dǎsuàn	15
大	dà	8
大概	dàgài	16
大家	dàjiā	18
大学	dàxué	15
但是	dànshì	13
蛋糕	dàngāo	12
当	dāng	15

279

到	dào	9		发	fā	16
的	de	3		翻译	fānyì	15
得	de	18		饭菜	fàncài	13
灯	dēng	17		方便	fāngbiàn	17
登记	dēngjì	20		非常	fēicháng	13
等	děng	20		丰富	fēngfù	19
地铁	dìtiě	14		风景	fēngjǐng	14
地址	dìzhǐ	17		服务	fúwù	17
点	diǎn	12		服装店	fúzhuāngdiàn	19
点钟	diǎnzhōng	16		付	fù	11
电话	diànhuà	12		附近	fùjìn	17
电脑	diànnǎo	16		复习	fùxí	16
电视	diànshì	14				
电影	diànyǐng	19		**G**		
东边	dōngbian	17		干净	gānjìng	9
懂	dǒng	19		感兴趣	gǎn xìngqù	18
都	dōu	6		刚	gāng	17
对	duì	7		高	gāo	15
对	duì	18		高大	gāodà	20
多	duō	13		高兴	gāoxìng	6
多少	duōshao	7		哥哥	gēge	10
				歌	gē	12
E				个	gè	7
儿子	érzi	13		个子	gèzi	15
而且	érqiě	19		给	gěi	11
二	èr	5		跟	gēn	14
F				跟	gēn	18

公共汽车	gōnggòng qìchē	14
公司	gōngsī	10
拐	guǎi	17
关系	guānxi	13
关心	guānxīn	13
逛	guàng	16
国	guó	5
国家	guójiā	7

H

还	hái	14
还是	háishi	11
孩子	háizi	14
汉语	Hànyǔ	2
好	hǎo	1
好处	hǎochù	19
好好儿	hǎohāor	19
号	hào	12
合适	héshì	20
和	hé	6
很	hěn	2
红	hóng	11
红绿灯	hónglǜdēng	17
后边	hòubian	8
湖	hú	14
互相	hùxiāng	13
护照	hùzhào	20

花儿	huār	14
花园	huāyuán	20
画	huà	10
画儿	huàr	10
环境	huánjìng	20
黄	huáng	8
黄色	huángsè	8
回	huí	4
会	huì	18
或者	huòzhě	14

J

几	jǐ	3
寄	jì	17
价格	jiàgé	20
健康	jiànkāng	13
教	jiāo	7
角	jiǎo	11
叫	jiào	6
教室	jiàoshì	4
节	jié	9
斤	jīn	11
今年	jīnnián	7
今天	jīntiān	3
进	jìn	3
经常	jīngcháng	16
经理	jīnglǐ	10

酒店	jiǔdiàn	20
就	jiù	14
橘子	júzi	11
举行	jǔxíng	12
觉得	juéde	19

K

开始	kāishǐ	16
看	kàn	8
可爱	kě'ài	14
可是	kěshì	19
可以	kěyǐ	14
刻	kè	16
客气	kèqi	3
课	kè	3
空气	kōngqì	14
空儿	kòngr	14
口语	kǒuyǔ	7
块	kuài	11
快递	kuàidì	17
快乐	kuàilè	12
困	kùn	18

L

篮球	lánqiú	16
老师	lǎoshī	5
累	lèi	13
离	lí	17

礼物	lǐwù	12
里	lǐ	14
里边	lǐbian	17
练习	liànxí	16
两	liǎng	7
聊天儿	liáo tiānr	14
了解	liǎojiě	18
零	líng	5
留学生	liúxuéshēng	5
楼	lóu	8
旅行	lǚxíng	20

M

妈妈	māma	10
麻烦	máfan	19
马路	mǎlù	17
马上	mǎshàng	19
吗	ma	2
满意	mǎnyì	20
忙	máng	2
毛	máo	11
每	měi	13
妹妹	mèimei	10
门口	ménkǒu	17
米	mǐ	17
名字	míngzi	6
明天	míngtiān	5

N

哪	nǎ	8
哪里	nǎli	18
哪儿	nǎr	4
那	nà	6
那儿	nàr	8
南边	nánbian	17
难	nán	2
呢	ne	14
能	néng	18
你	nǐ	1
你们	nǐmen	7
年	nián	5
您	nín	6
牛奶	niúnǎi	11
努力	nǔlì	10

P

排	pái	20
排球	páiqiú	18
牌子	páizi	19
跑步	pǎo bù	16
陪	péi	15
朋友	péngyou	6
朋友圈儿	péngyouquānr	16
啤酒	píjiǔ	12
片	piàn	20

平常	píngcháng	16
苹果	píngguǒ	11
瓶	píng	11

Q

骑	qí	14
起床	qǐ chuáng	16
汽车	qìchē	14
千	qiān	9
前边	qiánbian	17
前天	qiántiān	19
钱	qián	11
请	qǐng	3
请问	qǐngwèn	8
取件	qǔ jiàn	17
去	qù	4
去年	qùnián	15

R

让	ràng	19
人	rén	5
认识	rènshi	6
日	rì	12
入住	rùzhù	20

S

散步	sàn bù	14
扫码	sǎo mǎ	11
色	sè	8

商场	shāngchǎng	16		她们	tāmen	13
商店	shāngdiàn	10		太	tài	2
上	shàng	16		特别	tèbié	18
谁	shéi	7		踢	tī	18
什么	shénme	4		体育馆	tǐyùguǎn	17
生活	shēnghuó	13		填	tián	17
生日	shēngrì	5		跳舞	tiào wǔ	12
十月	shíyuè	5		听	tīng	16
时候	shíhou	9		听力	tīnglì	7
食堂	shítáng	4		听说	tīngshuō	18
是	shì	4		图书馆	túshūguǎn	8
手续	shǒuxù	20		退换	tuìhuàn	19
售货员	shòuhuòyuán	10			W	
书	shū	3		外边	wàibian	17
书包	shūbāo	6		外文	wàiwén	9
树	shù	14		玩儿	wánr	7
树木	shùmù	20		晚	wǎn	10
水果	shuǐguǒ	11		晚会	wǎnhuì	12
睡	shuì	18		晚上	wǎnshang	8
顺便	shùnbiàn	20		万	wàn	9
送	sòng	12		网	wǎng	16
宿舍	sùshè	4		往	wǎng	17
岁	suì	7		微信	wēixìn	11
	T			位	wèi	7
他	tā	6		喂	wèi	14
他们	tāmen	7		文化	wénhuà	18

文章	wénzhāng	19		星期五	xīngqīwǔ	3
我	wǒ	4		星期一	xīngqīyī	3
我们	wǒmen	7		兴趣	xìngqù	18
午饭	wǔfàn	14		姓	xìng	6

X

				选	xuǎn	19
西边	xībian	17		学	xué	18
西瓜	xīguā	11		学生	xuésheng	6
喜欢	xǐhuan	6		学习	xuéxí	5

Y

下	xià	15		样子	yàngzi	19
下单	xià dān	17		要	yào	11
下午	xiàwǔ	8		一	yī	5
下载	xiàzài	17		一边	yìbiān	19
现在	xiànzài	5		(一)点	(yì) diǎnr	11
香水	xiāngshuǐ	15		一共	yígòng	11
小学	xiǎoxué	15		一起	yìqǐ	7
笑	xiào	19		一直	yìzhí	17
谢谢	xièxie	3		椅子	yǐzi	9
新	xīn	8		音乐	yīnyuè	16
新闻	xīnwén	16		饮料	yǐnliào	12
信息	xìnxī	20		英文	Yīngwén	8
星期	xīngqī	3		英语	Yīngyǔ	3
星期二	xīngqī'èr	3		用	yòng	14
星期六	xīngqīliù	3		用品	yòngpǐn	19
星期三	xīngqīsān	3		邮件	yóujiàn	19
星期四	xīngqīsì	3		有	yǒu	3
星期天	xīngqītiān	3				

有的	yǒude	13
有点儿	yǒudiǎnr	13
有名	yǒumíng	19
有意思	yǒu yìsi	10
又	yòu	17
右边	yòubian	10
语法	yǔfǎ	7
预习	yùxí	16
预约	yùyuē	17
元	yuán	11
远	yuǎn	8
阅览室	yuèlǎnshì	9
运动	yùndòng	18

Z

杂志	zázhì	9
再	zài	11
再见	zàijiàn	4
在	zài	8
在	zài	14
咱们	zánmen	19
早饭	zǎofàn	16
早上	zǎoshang	4
怎么	zěnme	11
怎么样	zěnmeyàng	13
展览	zhǎnlǎn	18
张	zhāng	9

找	zhǎo	11
照片儿	zhàopiānr	10
这	zhè	4
这儿	zhèr	9
正	zhèng	14
正在	zhèngzài	14
支付宝	zhīfùbǎo	11
只好	zhǐhǎo	19
中间	zhōngjiān	10
中文	Zhōngwén	8
中午	zhōngwǔ	8
种	zhǒng	9
周	zhōu	10
周围	zhōuwéi	20
主意	zhúyi	19
祝	zhù	12
桌子	zhuōzi	9
自己	zìjǐ	13
自行车	zìxíngchē	14
走	zǒu	17
足球	zúqiú	18
最后	zuìhòu	18
最近	zuìjìn	13
左边	zuǒbian	10
坐	zuò	14

专名

A

| 安达 | Āndá | 8 |
| 安德 | Āndé | 13 |

B

| 北京大学 | Běijīng Dàxué | 7 |
| 波伟 | Bōwěi | 6 |

D

| 丁荣 | Dīng Róng | 6 |

H

| 韩国 | Hánguó | 8 |
| 华联超市 | Huálián Chāoshì | 17 |

L

| 李明爱 | Lǐ Míng'ài | 8 |

M

| 美国 | Měiguó | 8 |

S

| 上海 | Shànghǎi | 17 |

T

| 泰国 | Tàiguó | 16 |
| 田 | Tián | 7 |

W

| 王 | Wáng | 7 |
| 王明 | Wáng Míng | 6 |

X

| 新街口 | Xīnjiēkǒu | 17 |

Y

| 英国 | Yīngguó | 5 |

Z

| 张 | Zhāng | 5 |

语法索引

	语法项目	课号	页码
C	称数法（1）：百以内的数字	7	97
	称数法（2）：百以上的数字	9	124
	程度补语（1）	19	261
	存在句	17	228
D	"的"字结构	11	145
	定语和助词"的"	8	111
	动词重叠	16	213
	动词谓语句	6	84
	动作的进行	14	190
F	方位词	17	230
G	概数的表达（1）：多（1）	9	123
H	号码的读法	16	215
J	兼语句	19	262
L	连动句	14	191
M	名词谓语句	12	159
N	"呢"和省略问句	16	214
	能愿动词（1）	18	244
	能愿动词（2）	19	260

语法项目	课号	页码
R		
人民币的表示法	11	145
日期表达法	12	158
S		
时刻表达法	16	216
"是"字句	6	85
数量词组	7	97
双宾语句	11	146
X		
相邻的两个数字表示概数	17	231
形容词谓语句	8	112
Y		
一边……一边……	19	263
疑问句（1）：用"吗"的疑问句	6	85
疑问句（2）：用"什么"提问	6	85
疑问句（3）：特指问句"多少""几"和"谁"	7	98
疑问句（4）：特指问句"哪儿""哪"	8	109
疑问句（5）：正反问句	9	123
疑问句（6）：选择问句"A 还是 B"	11	144
疑问句（7）：语调疑问句	12	158
疑问句（8）：用疑问代词"多"提问	13	175
疑问句（9）：……怎么样？	13	175
疑问句（10）：用"……，好吗"提问	14	192
疑问句（11）：用"怎么"提问	14	192
"有"字句	7	96
又……又……	17	231

	语法项目	课号	页码
Z	主谓谓语句	13	173
	状态补语（1）	18	246
	状语（1）：副词做状语	7	98
	状语（2）：时间状语和地点状语	12	159